Selected Works

Ricardo Santiago

Preface

Ricardo Santiago was an activist working toward the construction of an international socialist network capable of overturning the global capitalist system of exploitation. He produced numerous written materials in pursuit of that goal.

Over a period of years, he wrote on topics ranging from the situation in Korea to revolutions in places Afghanistan and Nicaragua and strikes in the United States.

Although he began to reconsider some of his positions as the organizations he belonged to collapsed, he never forsook socialism. His writings continue to retain historical, political and intellectual value.

1978 Saur Revolution in Afghanistan

In 1978 the Saur Revolution swept across the central Asian country of Afghanistan uprooting backwards social and property relations and liberating women from domestic slavery, abuse and extreme oppression.

Background

Afghanistan is a country with a long and complicated history. Throughout the years, it came under the influence of many different groups, from the Kushans to the Iranians to the Greeks to the Mongols.

The Durrani empire was established in 1747, with a man of Pashtun ethnicity named Ahmed Shah Durrani at its head. Besides a very short period in 1929 when a Khan named Bacha-i-Saqa briefly overthrew the government and named himself emir, every Afghan leader belonged to Ahmed Shah Durrani's tribal confederation.

In the nineteenth and early twentieth centuries the people of Afghanistan fought against the British imperialists several times resulting in various parts of the country falling under British control.

The borders of modern Afghanistan resulted from a combination of of those battles and competition between the British and Russian Empires.

In 1921, after army leader Amanullah Khan led a successful uprising, Afghanistan formally won its independence from the British.

In 1933, Mohammed Zahir Shah became king after his father was assassinated. He instituted a few reforms, such as limited education for women, but also showed great indifference towards the country's toilers, as could be expected.

While infrastructure crumbled and famine lead to thousands of starvation deaths, Zahir Shah used the country's resources to have castles built for himself in Kabul and Italy.

Zahir Shah ruled until 1973, when he was overthrown in a bloodless coup led by his cousin Mohammed Daoud Khan.

Instead of naming himself king, Daoud broke tradition and proclaimed Afghanistan a republic, with himself as president. He was originally backed by Parcham, a reformist faction of the People's Democratic Party of Afghanistan (PDPA), because he promised to introduce a number of progressive, democratic reforms.

Instead, Daoud's rule was marked by increasing repression, including the arrests and executions of numerous revolutionaries and the closure of the newspapers of both the Parcham and the more revolutionary Khalq factions of the PDPA.

The factions of the PDPA, which formed in 1965 and split from each other two years later, finally reunified in 1977, with the encouragement of the Communist Party of the Soviet Union.

The Saur Revolution

In late 1977, students and workers in the capital city of Kabul rose up against the oppressive Daoud government, but were put down by the police. After the rebellion, Daoud had several members of the PDPA jailed.

In January, 1978, another uprising broke out as thousands of Afghans demanded the release of the jailed PDPA members. The police were unable to put down the rebellion and so the army was called in to smash it.

A few months later, in March, Mir Akbar Khyber (also

known as "Kaibar"), a leading member of Parcham, was murdered by government forces. Tens of thousands of Afghans gathered soon after to listen to speeches delivered by leaders of the PDPA. Daoud was frightened by this display of popular support for the PDPA,and ordered its leaders imprisoned.

By the time the Daoud's forces had got around to jailing one PDPA leader, and putting another under house arrest, the Saur Revolution had already broken out.

PDPA members in the military, with the support of tens of thousands of others, began an uprising against the Daoud government on April 28, 1978.

The uprising started at the Kabul International Airport and spread to the capital of Kabal within twenty-four hours. It was there, on April 28, that revolutionary forces stormed the presidential palace and overthrew Mohammed Daoud Khan.

Upon taking power, the revolutionaries took to the radio to declare, "For the first time, power has come to the people. The last remnants of the imperialist tyranny, despotism and the royal dynasty have been ended."

Two days later, hundreds of thousands of Afghans marched through the streets waving red flags and celebrating the victory of the Saur Revolution.

Revolutionary measures

The revolutionaries moved quickly to establish the Democratic Republic of Afghanistan, with a Revolutionary Council at its head, and a provisional democratic program that guaranteed the legalization of trade unions, equal rights for women and the separation of church and state.

In the years leading up to the Saur Revolution Afghanistan was a reactionary nightmare for the large majority of its residents – especially women, who were fundamentally the property of their fathers or husbands to be bought and sold.

10

Prior to the Saur Revolution, there were only 35,000 workers employed in manufacturing in Afghanistan, while there were some 250,000 mullahs who existed as parasites living off the poor masses.

There were no railroad tracks or highways to speak of and malnutrition and starvation was the norm.

Only 10 percent of men and 2 percent of women could read.

The average person lived just 40 years, and half of all children died before reaching the age of five.

In contrast, in the neighboring Soviet Republic of Uzbekistan nearly 100 percent of the population was literate and life expectancy was 70.

The revolutionary Afghan government began carrying out revolutionary measures to combat the problems facing the toilers of Afghanistan almost immediately.

The first step was to construct schools and hospitals across the country, and to train doctors and teachers.

As Saira Noorani, a female Afghan doctor, recalled in the *Observer* in 2001, "Life was good ... Every girl could go to high school and university. We could go wherever we wanted and wear what we liked."

The revolutionary leadership also canceled the massive debts that the poor peasants owed to the loan sharks and landowners.

They also began a sweeping land reform policy, to take arable land out of the hands of the exploiting mullahs – who controlled 42 percent of it, and necessary irrigation systems, and put them into the hands of the peasantry that actually did the farming.

In doing this they met huge resistance from the mullahs who saw their easy ride on the backs on the poor coming to an

11

end.

The mullahs raised reactionary counterrevolutionary gangs that carried out vicious acts of terrorism and economic sabotage.

Despite this, the revolutionary government was still able to redistribute land to 200,000 landless peasants (in a country of 20 million).

But it was the revolution's establishment of equal rights for women – which included the establishment of compulsory schooling for young girls, and free literacy classes for adult women – that truly raised opposition from the mullahs, khans and strong Islamic clergy.

The counterrevolution

The reactionary 'mujahedin' (or holy warriors – the name that the bands of the khans, mullahs and Islamic clergy gave themselves) that lead the counterrevolution sought to preserve their positions in society. These position rested upon a backwards system in which women were the private property of men, where local laws only allowed married men access to land and water – with more wives meaning more of those resources, and where a price was literally put on each bride.

In these reactionaries the U.S. capitalist ruling elite saw an ally against the spread of revolution and the overthrow of capitalism internationally and Soviet Union itself, which bordered Afghanistan to the north.

It didn't take the U.S. imperialists long to began aiding the mujahedin secretly through the CIA, sending them money, guns, bombs, advisors, special agents and the like.

On top of this, the reactionary capitalist governments in Pakistan, Egypt and Saudi Arabia, along with the fraudulent bureaucrats that controlled China, were also aiding the counterrevolutionaries.

As the armed counterrevolution grew, with literally tons of aid pouring in from the CIA, China, Pakistan, Egypt and Saudi Arabia, Revolutionary Defense Groups were formed in Afghanistan, with the participation of large numbers of women who sought to defend the rights they had gained.

At the same time, the revolutionary government requested military assistance from the USSR.

The bureaucratic leadership of the USSR first sent only military advisers before finally being pressured by the reality of imperialist-backed counterrevolution at the gates of the Central Asian Soviet Republics to send in some 100,000 troops.

While revolutionary Afghanistan's army and popular militias, with the assistance of soldiers from the USSR, were more or less able to beat back the counterrevolutionaries for ten years, horrendous atrocities were still carried out.

Whenever the reactionaries of the mujahedin were able to get a hold of a soldier from the USSR or a teacher (who committed the "crime" of teaching a women to read), they would frequently cut up, skin or behead them, or some combination thereof. Other times they would drug them and imprison them, so that they could be brutally tortured later.

These savage reactionaries – which included amongst their ranks Osama bin Laden – were the people Democratic U.S. President Jimmy Carter gave billions of dollars to, and the same scum Republican U.S. President Ronald Reagan hailed as "freedom fighters."

USSR withdraw

In 1985, Mikhail Gorbachev became the leader of the Soviet Union.

Under the guise of "democratic reform" and "openness," Gorbachev and his cohorts sought to settle with the imperialists – who were openly driving for the destruction of the USSR –

and allow an increase in capitalist penetration.

On July 20, 1987, the USSR, then beginning to crumble under the weight of internal contradiction and the suicidal policies of its bureaucratic leadership, treacherously announced that it planned to withdraw all troops from Afghanistan.

By 1989 the task was complete, leaving the revolutionary Afghan government to stand on its own against a counterrevolutionary band receiving major backing from several governments.

At the time, there were over a quarter of a million women working, and another 15,000 women serving in the army and militias in Afghanistan. Women made up half of the doctors and university teachers in the country, and more than 500,000 were enrolled in schools and literacy programs. For the first time in the history of Afghanistan, women could walk around in the cities without having to wear a veil.

All of these women were prime targets for the reactionary mujahedin which, emboldened by the withdraw of the Soviets, were now stepping up their attacks.

In response to this serious threat, the PDPA set out to arm and train all of its female members.

More civil war

Despite the withdraw of the USSR, the revolutionary forces of Afghanistan were able to hold their own against the mujahedin reactionaries for some time.

In fact, the Afghan Army, which had been trained by the USSR's military and by participating in several battles, actually began to perform better after the USSR's withdraw.

The militias too did well against the counterrevolutionaries. They were able to successfully defend, for instance, the Afghan city of Jalalabad from the onslaught of mujahedin bands operating out of nearby CIA bases in Pakistan.

But the revolutionary forces, demoralized by the counterrevolutionary destruction of the USSR and under a *de facto* oil blockade from Russia's new capitalist government, were increasingly fractured and divided. By 1992 they could no longer hold out.

The counterrevolution succeeds

By April, 1992, the mujahedin entered the capital city of Kabu, and President Mohammad Najibullah was overthrown.

A "coalition" government was then set up, made up of elements of the mujahedin – which was beginning to split into different factions – some PDPA members, and some army officers.

Over the next four years control of the government would shift back and forth between different factions of the mujahedin, but one thing remained the same throughout: all the progressive measures introduced by the revolution were steadily being overturned.

In 1996, one particularly reactionary Islamic fundamentalist militia, the Taliban, was able to take control of Kabul, which was devastated by years of war.

One of the first acts the Taliban carried out was the forceful removal of Mohammad Najibullah from the UN compound he had been staying in. They then proceeded to publicly castrate him before hanging him and his brother from a lamp post in downtown Kabul where they were left for three days.

The aftermath

The rule of the Taliban, which enjoyed the support of the

U.S. imperialists that funded it as a part of the mujahedin early on, was notoriously oppressive.

Upon taking power, these reactionary religious extremists threw acid in the faces of women whose faces were uncovered, closed down schools and created groups of young thugs that went around brutally beating any woman who so much as bared her wrist.

Under their rule, women were forcefully secluded in their homes (where all windows had to be painted black). Women were forced to wear a burqa which covered them from head to toe, and were forbidden to be educated after the age of 8 (and prior to that, they could only learn about the Muslim holy book, the Qu'ran).

In 2001, the U.S. imperialists used the September 11 attacks on the World Trade Center and Pentagon as justification to invade Afghanistan and overthrow the Taliban, which had refused to bow to their demands.

Today, Afghanistan remains a horribly oppressive country, occupied by imperialist forces and headed by a U.S. puppet leader.

1965 Revolution in the Dominican Republic

In 1965, the workers and farmers of the Dominican Republic poured into the streets, arms in hand, with the goal of creating a truly democratic, independent country. Under the leadership of the heroic Francisco Caamaño, they successfully held off U.S.-backed right-wing forces, and even members of the U.S. military itself for some time, although unfortunately, they were eventually defeated.

Background

The Dominican Republic was colonized by the Spanish after Christopher Columbus landed there in 1492. Other than a few brief stints under French, Haitian and independent self-rule, the country effectively belonged to Spain until 1865. It was in that year that Dominican rebels finally won lasting independence after years of waging a "War of Restoration." But this independence did not last long, as the country traded one colonial power for another.

In 1905, the United States government took over the administration of the country's customs authority after several European powers sent warships to the capital city of Santo Domingo to demand repayment of loans given to the earlier government of Ulises 'Lilís' Heureaux. The U.S. Bureau of Insular Affairs gained receivership of Dominican customs and the U.S. became the sole foreign creditor of the country. It was through this act that the United States laid the ground work for turning the Dominican Republic into a neocolony, under its complete economic control.

Over the next few years, as various sections of the local rulers battled for control of the Dominican Republic, U.S.

capitalists poured money into the country's sugar cane industry. In 1914, U.S. President Woodrow Wilson demanded that a president be chosen, saying his country would impose one otherwise.

Heureaux-Juan Isidro Jimenes, a wealthy capitalist who made his money in the tobacco industry, was elected but faced demands that he appoint a director of public works and financial adviser from the United States and create a new military under the command of U.S. officers. The Dominican Congress refused these demands and began proceedings to impeach Jimenes. Desiderio Arias, the Minister of War, staged a coup in 1916, which the U.S. used as a pretext to invade.

On May 15, 1916, U.S. Marines landed in the Dominican Republic. After a brief period of fighting, they controlled the entire country. The Dominican Congress elected a President, but he was replaced by a U.S. military dictatorship after he refused to meet the demands of the U.S. For the next several years censorship was intense, critics of the foreign dictatorship were arrested, and individual peasants were forced off their lands to make way for the expansion of huge sugar plantations.

Throughout the U.S. occupation, bands of peasants from the eastern part of the country called *gavilleros* waged a guerrilla war against the occupiers. The U.S. created a National Police force, which still exists to this day, to fight the guerrillas.

The U.S. occupiers finally withdrew in 1924, but only after insuring all laws passed under their dictatorship would stay intact and control of Dominican customs would remain in their hands.

In May of 1930, Rafael Leonidas Trujillo, the leader of the 'Dominican National Guard' created under the U.S. occupation and self-described 'Number One Anticommunist', took power in a sham election. For the next three decades, this admirer of Hitler and Mussolini would rule over the country with U.S. backing, oppressing the population while enriching himself.

In 1961, the U.S. government became concerned that Trujillo's brutal rule would unite the workers and farmers of the Dominican Republic against him, prompting a revolution similar to the one that had occurred in nearby Cuba a few years earlier. On May 30, Trujillo was assassinated under the direction of the CIA.

The U.S. government then maneuvered Joaquín Balaguer, a protégé of Trujillo, into power. Popular pressure soon forced him into exile and brought new elections.

In those elections, which took place in 1962, Juan Bosch, a liberal poet and long time enemy of Trujillo was elected president.

Bosch carried out minor land distribution and nationalizations aimed at stemming the revolutionary aspirations of the Dominican Republic's workers and farmers, but also banned communist parties. But despite his allegiance to maintain capitalism, his refusal to unquestioning go along with the plans of the U.S. government was enough reason for them to remove him. A neocolony, even a capitalist one, attempting to determine its own future was simply intolerable.

In September of 1963, right wing officers in the military forced Bosch from power with full U.S. backing.

The revolution begins

After Bosch's ouster, the U.S. government helped set up a military dictatorship under the guise of a 'civilian triumvirate.'

This dictatorship was lead by General Elías Wessin y Wessin of the *Centro de Entrenamiento de las Fuerzas Armadas* (Armed Forces Training Center or "CEFA") – a 2,000 strong force of military specialists, originally established under Trujillo. Among its other repressive policies, the dictatorship proclaimed that "The Communist doctrine, Marxist-Leninist, Castroite, or whatever it is called, is now outlawed."

Workers continually carried out strikes in protest of the dictatorship until finallyon April 24, 1965, a group of soldiers, led by Colonel Francisco Caamaño, rose up and took control of the government. The soldiers and their supporters, known as *constitutionalistas* for their support of the constitution which had been scrapped upon Bosch's overthrow, took to the streets. Before long, they had seized all major television and radio stations, as well as the National Palace.

In the earliest stages, the demands of the *constitutionalistas* were simple: the restoration of the constitution and the return of the elected president. Instead of meeting the demands, the CEFA launched a counter attack, in which many workers and farmers were killed.

As the *constitutionalistas* took steps to defend themselves, through distributing arms to the general population and organizing organs of defense, they began to transform society. Through their struggle, the workers and farmers began to discover that the only way to make the country truly independent and democratic would be to take control of things themselves and break from the grips of imperialism.

Unwilling to risk another revolution in 'their backyard,' the U.S. imperialist rulers decided to act.

Initially, the U.S. established a military presence in the Dominican Republic by setting up a landing strip it claimed it would use to evacuate U.S. citizens from the country. As the rightists of the CEFA suffered defeat after defeat (resulting in their eventual withdrawal to their base in San Isidro), the U.S. beefed up its presence, sending in 42,000 soldiers and blockading the country with 41 warships – again under the pretense of 'protecting foreign citizens,' even though none had been killed or even injured.

The U.S. was then pressured some of its puppet governments throughout Latin America send in troops to help with the counterrevolution. On top of the tens of thousands of U.S. forces, several thousand arrived from Brasil, Honduras, Paraguay, Nicaragua, Costa Rica and El Salvador.

Stating the plain truth, Caamaño was quoted as saying "The war would be already over if the U.S. had not intervened."

The invaders were able to bring an end to the revolutionary government after a few months of fighting, mainly by cutting off the constitutionalistas in the capital through the creation of a fake, supposedly neutral "safety corridor."

Despite the fact that the revolutionary forces had been forced from power, resistance to the occupation continued for the duration, until the U.S. forces decided to allow supposedly "democratic" elections in 1966, in order to alleviate some of the anger of the Dominican people.

The aftermath

Joaquín Balaguer was returned to power in the fraudulent elections of 1966. Shortly thereafter a new constitution was put in place that officially guaranteed some democratic rights, though it was more often than not disregarded.

Balaguer was "elected" again in 1970 and 1974, both times after his armed thugs forced the main opposition to withdraw from the elections.

Balaguer, whose brutality rivaled that of his teacher Trujillo, sold off the country piecemeal to the highest bidder. Under his rule, paramilitary death squads targeted the slum-dwelling workers and farmers that made up the base of the revolutionary movement. His henchmen destroyed popular movements and workers organizations while U.S.-based capitalists bought up land and local industries.

As the *Wall Street Journal* reported on September 9, 1971, "the [U.S.] embassy has done nothing publicly to dissociate itself from the terror. The U.S. continues to provide substantial aid, training, equipment, and arms, to the Dominican police and army."

In 1975, Juan Bosch correctly stated "This country is not pro-American, it is United States property."

Caamaño returns

After the revolutionary government was brought to an end, Francisco Caamaño came under attack. After a series of threats on his life, he was violently attacked by armed thugs at the Hotel Matum in Santiago. Soon after, he fled the country, landing first in England, and later, revolutionary Cuba.

In 1973, after years of staying off the radar, Caamaño returned to the Dominican Republic by boat with a band of rebels who planned to start up a nationwide movement that would lead to the overthrow the hated Balaguer and the establishment of an independent, democratic republic.

The rebels quickly made their way to mountains. From there, they aimed to gradually link up with workers and farmers across the country and carry out a nationwide revolution. Unfortunately, things did not work out as planned. After a series of initial mishaps and weeks of brave fighting, Caamaño was martyred by Balaguer's repressive forces on February 16, 1973.

Today, Caamaño is a hero to the toiling Dominican masses, who see in him the sacrifice and struggle desperately needed to completely the tasks originally set out upon in 1965.

The struggle continues

Today, the Dominican Republic is not much better than it was under the rule of Balaguer, and in many ways, it's much worse.

Politically motivated murders by the repressive forces of the state and paramilitary thugs are the norm. Prisons are absolute hellholes and suspects are held over fires and smothered by police to elicit confessions. The situation for Haitians, most of whom come to work for slave wages on sugar plantations, are even worse, with many being beaten, raped, jailed and even killed.

Women, who make up most of the workers in the 'free trade zones' are often forced to work long shifts for pennies and are frequently sexually abused by their bosses. If they become pregnant, most are fired. Overtime is often mandatory, and doors are chained shut so workers cannot leave.

Workers across the country are fired, and even physically attacked, for attempting to form or join unions. Workers with known affiliations to unions have been blacklisted and some businesses refuse to recognize unions outright.

Around 30 percent of the population of the Dominican Republic live under the official poverty line, eking out a meager existence on less than $2 (USD) a day. One in ten Dominicans dwells in extreme poverty, living on even less. One in five Dominicans of working age is unemployed. Nearly one out of three workers under the age of 24 is unemployed.

There is only one doctor per every 949 people. Many lack access to clean water. Power outages lasting several hours occur on a regular basis.

Forty-seven of every 1,000 children born in the Dominican Republic die before reaching their first birthday. Tens of thousands of children work in sweatshops, on plantations and as prostitutes. Over 15 percent of the population cannot read or write.

The only future that millions of Dominicans see is through immigration to another country, usually the United States.

Revolution is the only solution

An alternative to participating in elections is needed to solve the immense problems of the Dominican Republic.

The first and most important task is to complete the tasks of the 1965 revolution and free the country from the domination of the U.S. imperialists by any means necessary.

As an immediate outgrowth of that, the oppressed and exploited masses must fight to take power and organize a truly democratic political and economic system. In other words, the working class must rule, instead of the U.S. capitalists ruling through their local agents. It is only under such a system that the issues facing the toiling masses of the Dominican Republic can properly be addressed.

The Overthrow of Salvador Allende

September 11, 2009, marks the 36th anniversary of the brutal overthrow of Salvador Allende, the democratically elected socialist president of Chile. Allende was overthrown in a military coup, led by General Augusto Pinochet, that had the full backing of the United States government.

Allende's beginnings

Salvador Allende was born on July 26, 1908, in Valparaíso, Chile. His petty bourgeois (middle class), radical-liberal family had a history of involvement in social struggles. His grandfather was a founder of the reformist Radical Party and the first public school in Chile (at a time when the Catholic Church controlled education). His father and uncles also belonged to the Radical Party.

Besides the influences of his family, Allende was also influenced by an anarchist shoemaker named Juan Demarchi. He became even more conscious while attending medical school, during which time he lived in very poor conditions with a group of students who often read and discussed books by revolutionaries like Karl Marx, Vladimir Lenin and Leon Trotsky.

During his time at college, he became an outspoken leader of the Chilean Student Federation, and participated in a number of protests against U.S.-backed dictator Carlos Ibáñez. This activity resulted in numerous arrests for the young Salvador.

After graduating from college in 1932, Allende had a difficult time finding work as a doctor because of his reputation as a radical. He finally found a job preforming autopsies on the corpses of the poor. Seeing so many dead as a result of curable diseases, simply because they could not afford treatment, further affected Allende.

Allende married Hortensia Bussi, who was herself related to Marmaduque Grove, a military general who lead a 1932 coup that resulted in the formation of the short lived "Socialist Republic of Chile" (June 4 – 16, 1932). Grove was also a founder of the Socialist Party of Chile, which was formed in 1933. Allende was one of its first members.

Entering government

In 1937, Allende was elected to the Chilean National Congress. Soon after taking office, he introduced a number of bills on public healthcare, welfare and the rights of women.

He served as Minister of Health in the "Popular Unity" government (made up of the Socialist Party, Communist Party, Radical Party, Social Democratic Party and the Popular Unitary Action Movement) in both 1939 and 1941.

While serving in this position, he released a book entitled "The Chilean Socio-Medical Reality." This book explained how certain health issues (infant and maternal mortality, tuberculosis, infectious diseases, etc.) prevalent among the working class were caused by their poor living conditions, and argued for serious steps to be taken to rectify the problem. Instead of a strictly medical approach, he proposed social changes (redistribution of housing and land, income redistribution, improving workers' wages and workplace safety, etc.) that could get to the root of the problem.

In 1942, Allende became the leader of the Socialist Party and was elected to the Chilean Senate. Not long after, he introduced legislation that would create a national health care service. After its approval, Chile became the first country in the Americas to make health care available to all of its citizens (something most of the countries in the Western Hemisphere still haven't done).

He remained in the Senate (reelected several times), while running for president in 1952, 1958 and 1964. After his three unsuccessful bids for the presidency, he joked that his head stone would read "Here lies the next president of Chile."

But Allende was gaining popularity. In each election, he gained more votes than he had in the last. The imperialist U.S. government was becoming worried. In 1959, a year after almost winning the presidential election in Chile, Allende traveled to Cuba, where Fidel Castro, Ernesto "Che" Guevara and others had recently lead a revolution that ousted U.S.-backed dictator Fulgencio Batista. While there, he befriended Fidel and Raul Castro, and received a copy of Che's book "Guerrilla Warfare" which contained an inscription that read: "To Salvador Allende, who is trying to obtain the same result by other means, Affectionately, Che."

Allende, a socialist, friend of the Cuban Revolution, and supporter of communist guerrilla movements across Latin America as well as Che Guevara, who was murdered while leading a guerrilla war in Bolivia in 1967, looked like he may become the next president of Chile.

If that happened, the U.S. government feared, several of the capitalist exploiters it represented, such as the owners of the ITT, Anacoda and Kennecott corporations – who were heavily invested in the country – might have their factories nationalized. On top of this, the election of Allende would interfere with the U.S. government's attempts to isolate Cuba, and turn back its revolution.

Furthermore, if the events lead to a socialist revolution in which the local capitalist rulers and imperialist lackeys were overthrown by the working class, it would open the doorway to similar events throughout Latin America.

Preemptive strike

The U.S. government, through its various agencies, went

into full gear to prevent the election of Salvador Allende in the 1970 elections.

Through, and with the cooperation of ITT and other channels, the CIA illegally funded the election campaign of right-wing capitalist Jorge Alessandri, the incumbent who Allende was running against. (This was nothing new. In 1964 they had done the same thing, funneling large sums of money to Allende's then-opponent.)

The CIA launched a program called "FUBELT," aimed at preventing Allende from becoming elected, or failing that, bring his time in office to a rapid conclusion.

In a document dated September 17, 1970 (now available in the U.S. National Security Archives) describing the results of a meeting between CIA chief Richard Helms and National Security Adviser Henry Kissinger, instructions for CIA operatives were laid out. "President Nixon had decided that an Allende regime in Chile was not acceptable to the United States.. The President asked the Agency to prevent Allende from coming to power or to unseat him. The President authorized ten million dollars for this purpose, if needed."

Despite all of this, the Chilean voters elected Allende in a three-way race (a liberal candidate from the Christian Democratic Party was also running). A section of the opposition to Allende argued for a run off election since Allende got less than 50 percent of the votes, even though there was no mention of the need for such in the constitution. In response, the National Congress took up the question.

In the meantime, the capitalist media went to work trying to whip up opposition to Allende's soon-to-be presidency. The cover of TIME magazine's October 19, 1970 issue (published only days before Allende's election was to be made official) read "Marxist Threat In The Americas – Chile's Salvador Allende."

Still, not everyone was fooled. One reader, in a letter to

the editor published in the next issue, wrote: "Sir: Intrigued by your marvelous cold war headline, MARXIST THREAT IN THE AMERICAS, I read on to see who is being threatened. Apparently it's some U.S. copper firms, the telephone company, and assorted juntas. Somehow, I'm not alarmed. I am, however, irritated by your persistent assumption that any form of Marxism enjoying any form of success in any part of the world is, *ipso facto*, a threat. This kind of thinking gave us Viet Nam. And it ignores the obvious: non-Marxist politicians have generally failed to meet the needs of the masses. I suggest we let our humanity transcend our cold war reflexes and hope that the people of Latin America are finding some kind of solution to their problems. We haven't been much help."

The CIA's work continued as well. Another secret CIA document dated October 16, 1970 read in part, "It is firm and continuing policy that Allende be overthrown by a coup. It would be much preferable to have this transpire prior to 24 October [the date Allende's election would be ratified] but efforts in this regard will continue vigorously beyond this date."

Chile's workers and farmers were outraged by the delay and the idea that the man they had elected may not take office. Allende himself warned "Santiago (Chile's capital) will be painted red with blood if I am not ratified as President."

Finally, and in spite of all the maneuvering on the part of the imperialists and their representatives and agents, the National Congress was forced by popular pressure to declare Salvador Allende President of Chile on October 24, 1970.

Imperialist aggression in full effect

Allende took office on November 3. Twelve days earlier, General René Schneider, Commander in Chief of Chile's army, was killed while resisting a kidnapping attempt by another group of soldiers under the leadership of Roberto Viaux. The kidnapping attempt was a part of a plan promoted by the CIA to carry out a coup before Allende could take office. Schneider had to be removed because he was fully opposed any violation of the constitution, such as a coup; but he wasn't supposed to be killed. Schneider's murder drew popular outrage, and forced the Viaux clique to abandon their plans.

With plans for a coup temporarily defeated, and the workers and farmers emboldened, Allende went to work. Diplomatic relations were immediately established with Cuba (in spite a U.S.-pushed Organization of American States convention forbidding countries in the Western Hemisphere from doing so) and the USSR, the People's Republic of China was recognized (for the first time by any country in South America), and a number of social programs were established.

The first steps were taken on the "Chilean road to socialism."

Foreign owned banks, copper and coal mines, and steel and iron mills were nationalized.

In the nationalized industries and public works projects which were launched, employment was made available for the poor and unemployed. As a result, the unemployment rate was cut in half.

The healthcare and education systems were put taken over by the government and opened to the public.

Free milk, which many could not afford previously, was provided to each child to prevent malnutrition.

Large estates were broken up and redistributed to those without land.

Prices on essential products were frozen, while at the same time workers were given raises.

Taxes were reformed so that the poorest of the poor wouldn't have to shoulder the burden.

Hundreds of thousands of retirees had their pensions

raised.

A state of the art networked of telex machines and computers was installed that allowed factories to communicate with each other in real time, thus facilitating planned production.

Workers and farmers were mobilized. Landless farmers began to occupy land, and industrial workers began to take over their workplaces. Industrial output increased by 14 percent.

In 1971, Cuban revolutionary Fidel Castro was invited to Chile. He spent several weeks there, holding a number of public rallies, which drew huge crowds, and giving the socialist members of Chile's government advice.

In response to the events in Chile, the U.S. imperialists began a campaign of economic warfare, just as they had (and continue to do) with Cuba. President Richard Nixon demanded that his foot soldiers "make the [Chilean] economy scream." In line with this, U.S. Ambassador to Chile, Edward M. Korry, proclaimed, "Not a nut or bolt shall reach Chile under Allende. … we shall do all within our power to condemn Chile and all Chileans to utmost deprivation and poverty."

What about the "democracy" that the U.S. government has always claimed to uphold? Henry Kissinger made their position on that clear, saying "I don't see why we need to stand by and watch a country go communist due to the irresponsibility of its people. The issues are much too important for the Chilean voters to be left to decide for themselves."

This should come of no surprise. The same thing happened in Viet Nam. When the U.S. government realized that communist leader Ho Chi Minh was sure to win upcoming elections in that country, they canceled them! In the same vein, they sponsored a coup against democratically elected Venezuelan President Hugo Chavez just a few years ago (though a mass mobilization prevented its success).

Besides cutting off trade, credit and aid to Chile, the

U.S. government sponsored publications, television and radio broadcasts that slandered Allende and worked to destabilize the country. Among other things, they claimed Allende and the Popular Unity government were puppets of the USSR (just as they had done with Cuba), even though this was clearly not the case. Although Allende maintained friendly relations with the Soviet Union, he didn't take orders from its leadership. This was made obvious during his time as a Senator, during which he openly denounced its invasions of Hungary and Czechoslovakia.

Of course, like democracy, the U.S. government is only concerned with the truth when it serves the interests of the capitalist ruling class.

Problems arise

Things were far from perfect under Allende, though the imperialists had as much to do with that as anything.

The imperialists and local capitalists had begun withdrawing their investments from the country as soon as Allende was elected. This only increased as it became clear that the oppressed and exploited were on the move.

The moves by the U.S. government and its agents to "make the economy scream" began to take their toll. Aid from the U.S., which had amounted to $1 billion (US) during the six-year presidency of Alessandri alone, disappeared after Allende took office.

Trade was limited or refused by the U.S. and its puppets, causing exports to fall by 24 percent. At the same time, a slight drop in agricultural output (which was expected for a short period while land was redistributed) made it necessary to increase imports by 26 percent.

Shortages and inflation led to the creation of a black market, leading to even more problems.

On top of all this, the price of copper, Chile's main export, which was set internationally, fell from $66 (U.S.) per ton in 1970 to $48 in 1972. This meant a major loss of funds for the country.

Often with direct U.S. assistance, and always with its backing, the capitalists and their agents in Chile launched a serious of "strikes" and lockouts. Through intimidation, blackmail and deception, they were able to get teachers and other workers to walk off the job, bringing the economy to a halt. Elements of the petty bourgeoisie, like private physicians (who were angry about the Socialist government's programs of public health, which meant less money for them), truck owners, and store owners followed suit.

Through all this, Allende's popularity continued to grow. In the March 1973 elections, the Popular Unity coalition gained more votes that it had when Allende came into office.

Still, the economic crisis facing the country, and the failure of the Popular Unity government to arm the country's workers and farmers, led to conditions favorable to the imperialists and their allies.

On June 29, 1973, another coup attempt, known as el Tanquetazo (the tank putsch), was launched. Under the leadership of leading members of a right-wing fascist group called "Fatherland and Liberty," a force made up of several tanks and dozens of soldiers made its way toward La Moneda (the presidential residence), with the aim of overthrowing Allende and installing a military dictatorship.

Early in the morning hours the coup plotters began firing on La Moneda and the Ministry of Defense. Several workers were killed during the attack.

Allende gave a radio broadcast in which he promised to defend the constitution to the end, while calling on workers to occupy the factories "and be ready in case it is necessary to fight alongside the soldiers of Chile."

General Carlos Prats, along with others in the military, drew up a plan to counter the advance. Within an hour, they began to move in.

When his group reached the area around La Moneda, Prats made a bold decision. Instead of waging all out warfare, he, along with two others, simply marched up to the tanks outside and commanded those in them to come down and surrender. This process continued to work until one tank operator shouted "I will not surrender General," while pointing the tank's barrel at Prats and his group. While the two went back and forth, Major Osvaldo Zabala sneaked up behind the tank operator and pointed a rifle at his head, forcing him to give up. More units began to arrive on the scene, including one under the command of Augusto Pinochet himself, future leader of yet another coup. The soldiers that had taken part in the plan to overthrow Allende ran away as fast as they could.

During these events, a large crowd had come to La Moneda to show their support for Allende. He delivered a speech to them, in which he explained what was going on, and asked them to remain calm and continuing to trust in the government.

The coup was smashed, but the threat of another still loomed.

At this time, Allende made a fatal error. He brought leading members of the armed forces into his Cabinet, hoping to win their support.

Soon after, a strange incident involving a traffic incident and protests by military officers pressured General Prats, who was then Interior minister and as Commander in Chief of the Army, to resign. In his place, he recommended Augusto Pinochet, then a General Chief of Staff of the Army.

On August 22, 1973, the Christian Democratic Party – which had earlier campaigned on a "socialist" platform, only to ally with right-wing forces after Allende's election – didn't wait long to make a move. In control of the Chamber of Deputies (after forming a bloc with the right-wing National Party), they were able to push through a resolution (though they lacked the two thirds majority required by the constitution to convict a president of abuse of power) which formally called for another military coup.

The resolution, entitled "Declaration of the Breakdown of Chile's Democracy," claimed that Allende had "the goal of establishing a totalitarian system."

So, to "save democracy," they called on the Military to overthrow a democratically elected president; and that's exactly what happened.

The other 9/11

On the morning of September 11, 1973, sections of the Chilean Navy seized the port city of Valparaíso, marking the beginning of a third coup.

As soon as Allende found about the morning's events, he rushed to La Moneda. With a handful of aides and members of the presidential guard by his side, he prepared for yet another showdown.

It wasn't long before members of "the Carabineros," Chile's national police, were surrounding La Moneda. Allende got to work trying to reach some of the generals of the various branches of the armed forces; but he was unable to get in contact with any of them.

"No one is answering. I think that this time all of them are involved," he remarked to his aides. He was right.

Soon after, President Allende broadcast a message to the people of Chile over the radio.

"Confirmed reports indicate that a sector of the Navy has rebelled and is occupying Valparaíso. Santiago is normal and [the soldiers are] in their barracks. I'm here defending the government that I represent by the will of the people. Be alert and vigilant... I wait for the soldiers of Chile to respond positively and defend the laws and the Constitution. Workers must go to their workplace and wait for new instructions," he said.

Allende also got in touch with Rolando Calderón, Secretary General of the CUT (Central Única de Trabajadores), one of the largest unions in the country. He asked Calderón to mobilize the workers in his union to shut down the radio stations broadcasting messages in support of the coup; but this was not done.

Instead, the coup leaders acted first, seizing and shutting down all radio stations supportive, or even neutral, towards Allende.

At 8:40 AM, a radio broadcast was made announcing the coup and its supposed intentions. Augusto Pinochet Ugarte, Commander in Chief of the Army; José Toribio Merino, Commander in Chief of the Navy; Gustavo Leigh, commander in Chief of the Air Force, and César Mendoza Durán, Director General of Carabineros attached their names to the broadcast, signaling their aim to set themselves up as a new ruling junta.

Soon after the broadcast was made, the Carabineros began to withdraw from their positions around La Moneda, and an offer was made to Allende by the coup plotters. There was an airplane ready to take Allende and his family out of the country and to safety; but he'd have to resign as president. He flatly refused.

"I will not surrender, nor resign," he said.

Allende then made a final radio broadcast, through the one pro-Allende station that had not yet been shut down. "This will surely be the last time I speak to you," he said. "Magallanes Radio will be silenced, and the reassuring tone of my voice will not reach you. It doesn't matter. You will continue hearing it. I will always be with you. At the least, your memory of me will be that of a man who was loyal to the country... The people ought to defend themselves, but not sacrifice themselves. The people ought not let themselves be subdued or persecuted, but neither should they humble themselves... I have faith in Chile and its destiny. Other people will be able to transcend this sad and bitter moment, when treason tries to force itself upon us... I'm sure that my sacrifice will not be in vain... Long live Chile! Long live the people! Long live the workers!"

While the president's message was broadcast, a number of tanks began to approach, then attack, La Moneda.

Allende threw on an army helmet and grabbed the AK-47 rifle given to him by Fidel Castro. By his side stood just over a hundred supporters, many who were workers. They had a few small weapons, and a handful of bazookas and 30 caliber machine guns; but they were no match for the military forces descending on the building.

The soldiers fired tank and machine guns at La Moneda, shattering windows and destroying whole walls. A team in a helicopter patrolled the surrounding area, taking out workers and farmers who had acted as snipers, firing from buildings in defense of the president.

After a short while, there was a cease fire as Allende asked his supporters to lay down their weapons and surrender. Most of those by his side, including his two daughters, left the building. As the end of the evacuation drew near, fighter jets approached. They proceeded to bomb La Moneda, blowing doors off the hinges and smashing the few windows that were still intact. Helicopters then moved in on the building, firing tear gas canisters.

This was followed by a renewal of the ground attack. As tanks fired, a group of soldiers stormed the door of La Moneda and took the first floor. When Allende learned of the events, he ordered those remaining by his side on the second floor to put down their weapons and leave. Allende proceeded to Independence Hall, where he sat down, put his rifle between his legs, and fired two shots into his brain. This was the end of the democratically elected president of Chile, Salvador Allende. It was also the beginning of a vicious reign of terror that would last close to two decades.

Pinochet's reign of terror

Once the coup plotters were in full control, Augusto Pinochet declared himself chairman of the junta. He moved quickly to consolidate his rule.

All parties that belonged to the Popular Unity government were banned, along with all leftist and labor organizations.

On September 12, 1973, one day after the overthrow of Allende, thousands of Chileans were rounded up and taken to the Chile Stadium in Santiago. For their support of Allende they were tortured and beaten.

Victor Jara, a beloved musician, had every bone in his hands broken by Pinochet's thugs. As he lay on the ground, his captors mockingly suggested he play them a song. In response, he sung a song supportive of the overthrown Popular Unity government. He was immediately beaten, and then killed by machine gun fire.

A similar fate was shared by at least 3,000 other Chileans over the next seventeen years. More than 30,000 were tortured by Allende's military and secret police (known as DINA). Several thousands more were forced into exile to escape the repression.

Some of those who were able to escape were tracked down and murdered by DINA, which cooperated with the military dictatorships in Brazil, Paraguay, Uruguay and Argentina and the United States government through

"Operation Condor," a plan to wipe all opposition to imperialism in Latin American off the face of the earth.

Some 30,000 people were "disappeared" under the Operation, which went as far as assassinating Orlando Letelier, a former foreign minister under Salvador Allende, while he was on his way to his new job at the Institute of Policy Studies in Washington, DC, the capital of the United States.

In another particularly bloody incident in 1985, leftist professor José Manuel Parada, journalist Manuel Guerrero, and another Chilean named Santiago Nattino were beheaded by uniformed police at the behest of the military dictatorship.

Along side the repression instituted by Chile's new military regime came unrestricted capitalism. Guided by University of Chicago trained economists, Pinochet instituted a number of "reforms" that spelled disaster for the millions of Chilean workers and farmers.

Pinochet sold nationalized industries, banks and even the pension system to the highest bidder, abolished minimum wage, abolished union rights and seriously reduced taxes on the rich.

The result? Unemployment, which had fallen to 4.4 percent under Allende, jumped to over 30 percent, marking the highest increase ever in Latin American history.

The price of exports fell, as did real wages for workers, while poverty, homelessness, starvation and infant mortality rose dramatically.

This is the "democracy" the CIA-backed coup of 1973 brought to Chile.

In place of the democratically elected Allende, who had allowed his political opposition to participate in government, stood a military dictator who bellowed "not a leaf moves in Chile if I don't know about it!"

Augusto Pinochet remained in power until 1990, when

he stepped down after popular resistance forced him to hold a plebiscite, which he lost, in 1988. The brutal dictator remained Commander-in-Chief of the Army for another ten years and became a "Senator-for-life," under a clause created in the constitution which was rewritten under his rule, after that.

Pinochet the butcher died of congestive heart failure and pulmonary edema in December, 2006.

Allende's legacy & lessons for today

The events of September 11, 1973, were tragic, but not inevitable.

In order for us to move forward today, we must draw the lessons of events like these. From these lessons we must develop new strategies and tactics, to better enable us to defeat the handful of capitalist exploiters that run the world once and for all.

From the beginning of Allende's presidency and before, when the class struggle came out into the open, confrontations between the working class and the local capitalist ruling class and foreign imperialists steadily increased.

While the Popular Unity government's reforms most definitely benefited the working class, small farmers and women, and gave them more room to maneuver, they weren't enough.

The Popular Unity Government's "Chilean path to socialism" was based on a supposed "gradual transformation" of capitalism into socialism; but as Karl Marx, the "father" of communism who first discovered the laws of evolution in human history, pointed out, this is simply not possible.

Speaking of the Paris Commune, the revolutionary uprising in France in 1871 in which workers took power for the first time in history, Marx wrote, "One thing especially was proved by the Commune, viz., that 'the working class cannot simply lay hold of the ready-made state machinery, and wield it for its own purposes,"

In other words, you can't elect socialism, a classless society in which the needs of all are met.

In order establish socialism, the working class must rise up, smash the capitalist state apparatus and take control of the tools and technology used to satisfy the wants and needs of humanity.

While supporting the gains made by workers under the Paris Commune, Marx was also critical of its errors (some of which have since been duplicated).

For instance, Marx criticized the Communards' refusal to respond to attacks by the capitalist rulers of France with attacks of its own: "In their reluctance to continue the civil war opened by Thiers' [leader of the rest of France] burglarious attempt on Montmartre, the Central Committee [elected leadership body of the Paris Commune] made themselves, this time, guilty of a decisive mistake in not at once marching upon Versailles [another major city in France where Theirs and his forces had gathered after being driven from Paris by its workers], then completely helpless, and thus putting an end to the conspiracies of Thiers and his Rurals."

Here, Marx was saying that when workers take power, they shouldn't, and can't, be afraid to fight back when attacked by the capitalists seeking to restore their control.

Indeed, as a result of the gains they had made under Allende, the Chilean workers were not afraid to respond to such attacks. When the capitalists called strikes, workers organized manufacturing and transportation without them. They also took over workplaces and even formed workplace and farm councils.

But while these bodies should have been strengthened and supported as the basis for a new, workers' state, they were not.

In fact, the workers were often disarmed in the face of attacks by leaders who told them put their faith in the government, instead of relying on their own power.

So, while the efforts of the imperialists and local capitalists played a major part, we must admit that the main cause of the defeat of the movement in Chile was its leadership's "reluctance to continue the civil war opened by" the bourgeoisie and imperialists. This was not solely the fault of Allende, but also other socialists, communists, union leaders, etc., who promoted the non-existent electoral path to socialism.

The best way for us to remember the defeat of the Chilean movement, the overthrow of Allende, and the deaths, tortures and "disappearances" of thousands of our class brothers and sisters which occurred as a result of the U.S.-backed coup in Chile on September 11, 1973, is to continue to fight.

Today, we must join our Chilean brothers and sisters in the fight for world revolution, to bring an end to exploitation, wage-slavery, oppression, sexism, racism and all the other ills and miseries which result from the outdated capitalist system.

Who Was Che Guevara?

You've probably seen his face on t-shirts, hats, or some other piece of merchandise, but what do you really know about Che Guevara? What did he accomplish that made him the hero of oppressed people all around the world?

The Russian revolutionary Vladamir Lenin once pointed out the tendency of the ruling class to "co-opt" revolutionaries after their deaths, turning them into mere "logos" which they attempt to render meaningless by separating the individual from what it is they stood for. It is in an effort to combat this that we offer this article.

Of course, it is not within the scope of this article to completely detail the life of Che – that has already been attempted to varying degrees of success in numerous biographies – rather, we hope to to provide a general outline to those unfamiliar with the man, in hopes that it will lead them to dig deeper into the story of his life, his theories, and most importantly what he fought for: the liberation of humankind.

Early Years

Ernesto Guevara (the 'Che' part wouldn't come until much later) was born in Rosario, Argentina, in 1928. His mother and father could be described as middle-class, with liberal inclinations.

Even as a young boy, Guevara was known for his often radical perspective, but they wouldn't develop fully until later in life.

He suffered from crippling asthma from birth, so much so that his family had to relocate because of it, but it didn't stop him from becoming an excellent athlete. Rugby was one of the sports that he enjoyed most. His aggressive style of play earned him the nickname 'Fuser'.

In 1948, he enrolled in the University of Buenos Aires to study medicine. He was an excellent student who excelled at his studies.

The Journey Begins

In 1951, on the suggestion of his older friend, Alberto Granado, a biochemist, he decided to take a year off from school to embark on trip across South America that they had dreamed of taking for years. Guevara and his 29-year-old friend set off from their hometown of Alta Gracia on a 1939 Norton 500 cc motorcycle they called La Poderosa II (literally, "the mighty one"). As a part of their trip, they planned to spend a few weeks volunteering at the San Pablo leper colony in Peru. Guevara documented the trip in *The Motorcycle Diaries*, which was translated into English in 1996, and turned into a motion picture of the same name in 2004.

During the trip, Ernesto witnessed first hand many things that he hadn't had much experience with before, such as the widespread poverty and oppression faced by the masses of people throughout the Latin America (and the world) under capitalism. It was through this, as well as studies of the writings of revolutionaries like Karl Marx, that he began to understand that the only remedy to these ills lay in socialist revolution.

Through his trip he also began to see Latin America not as a grouping of separate nations divided by invisible, often imposed borders, but rather as a single cultural and economic entity. It was from this foundation that he began to formulate his concept of a united Ibero-America, united "from Mexico to the Magellan straits", and bound together by a "single mestizo" culture.

Upon his return to Argentina, Guevara was anxious to continuing traveling throughout Latin America, and so he completed his medical studies as quickly as possible, finishing in March of 1953.

Imperialism in Guatemala

Following his graduation, Guevara again set out on the road, this time planning to travel through Central America. After much traveling, he finally ended up in Guatemala, where the popular reformist Jacobo Arbenz Guzman had been elected president. Arbenz was attempting to bring about a social change through various reforms – particularly land reform.

It was at this time that Guevara acquired the nickname that would follow him for the rest of his life. Friends in Guatemala began to refer to him as *"Che"* (pronounced "chay"), after an interjection (often used to get attention, such as "hey" or "wow", but also used like "friend" or "pal") commonly used by Argentinians such as himself.

At the time, 2% of the population of Guatemala controlled 74% of the land suitable to farming, and only used 12% of it. Arbenz planned to redistribute some of the unused land to the poor farmers of the country who made up the majority of its population, a plan that they greatly supported.

The U.S.-based United Fruit Company (UFC), the largest landowner in Guatemala, fully opposed the plan, even though it was paid $600,000 (based on land values it declared for tax purposes) for unused land that was seized as the plan began to be implemented.

The UFC had close ties with the U.S. government, and lobbied the CIA and the Eisenhower administration to take action. In 1954, the administration commissioned the CIA to overthrow democratically elected president Arbenz in a plan called Operation PBSUCCESS. The plan was a success and Arbenz was forced to flee the country on June 27th.

Following the overthrow, Che offered to fight, but Arbenz instructed his foreign supporters to leave the country. After spending some time in the Argentine consulate, Che headed to Mexico.

Witnessing the events that took place in Guatemala enabled Che to understand more than ever that the U.S. was an imperialist power that would always oppose any movements that attempted to solve problems like inequality and poverty that are endemic to Latin America and the rest of the third world. His understanding of socialism as the only answer to these problems grew even stronger.

Incidentally, the U.S. sponsored military dictatorship that replaced Arbenz turned out to be one of the most brutal regimes in world history.

The Cuban Revolution

It was in Mexico City that Che would meet brothers Raul and Fidel Castro. The two were in exile from Cuba after being freed – by popular demand – from a Cuban prison to which they were sentenced after leading a failed attack on a military garrison as a part of a larger plan to overthrow U.S. sponsored dictator Fulgencio Batista. The Castro brothers and others Cubans were planning to return to Cuba as a guerrilla force named the "26th of July Movement" (after the date of the original attack on the garrison). Che immediately hit it off with Fidel and agreed to join the expedition as a medic on the first night.

After a period of training, and even imprisonment by the Mexican authorities, Fidel, Che, and 80 others departed from Tuxpan, Veracruz, aboard the cabin cruiser *Granma* in November 1956. Che was the only non-Cuban on board.

Bad weather, and other problems, delayed their arrival by two days, and so an armed uprising in Santiago, which was aimed at drawing away the attention of Batista's troops, ended up only serving to put them on alert. They finally landed, 30 miles away from the point where weapons and reinforcements awaited them.

Almost immediately after pulling themselves ashore they were ambushed by the dictator's army. All but a handful of the guerrillas were killed. It was during this battle that Che made a crucial decision when, while retreating, he chose to pick up a box of ammunition instead of his medical bag. He later described the situation, "Perhaps this was the first time I was confronted with the real-life dilemma of having to choose between my devotion to medicine and my duty as a revolutionary soldier. Lying at my feet were a knapsack full of medicine and a box of ammunition. They were too heavy for me to carry both of them. I grabbed the box of ammunition, leaving the medicine behind."

Fidel, Raul, and Che were among the survivors who then made their way undetected into the rugged Sierra Maestra mountains. From here they built a strong support base amongst the region's poor farmers which would soon spread to working people across the country. The numbers of the Rebel Army grew as they continued to carry out successful attacks.

Throughout the revolution, Che continually exhibited great courage, combat and leadership skills, self-discipline, and boldness. He soon rose to the highest rank in the Rebel Army, *Comandante* (Major). In Late 1958, he lead his column through a long and arduous march to the city of Santa Clara, where they would soon take over after derailing an armored train filled with Batista's henchmen. This proved to be the final straw and the dictator was forced to flee the country. Guevara later recorded his memories of the two year struggle in a series of articles that would later be published as a book entitled *Reminiscences of the Cuban Revolutionary War.*

Revolutionary Government

On January 1st, 1959, the 26th of July Movement called for a general strike – to serve as a final blow – which lead to the victory of the revolution. For his part in the fighting Che was declared a "Cuban citizen by birth" and was appointed

Commander of the La Cabaña Fortress prison. Soon after he divorced his Peruvian wife, Hilda Gadea, the mother of his first child whom he married while in Guatemala. Later he would marry Aleida March, another fighter in the Rebel Army, with whom he would have 4 children.

During his six months at the prison, Che oversaw people's courts in which the Cuban people dished out revolutionary justice to brutal killers, rapists, and other war criminals that served Batista during the war.

Later, Che would become an official of INRA (the National Institute of Agrarian Reform), that carried out one of the most extensive land reforms ever seen. Large plantations were seized from big (often foreign owned) businesses and given to the poor farmers that actually worked them. An Urban Reform was also carried out in which all rents were lowered so that no renter would have to spend more than 10% of their income on housing, and, after a few years, would receive ownership of it. The mansions of the rich were turned over to the servants that worked in them and the government bought up homes which weren't being used (usually because the owners had several homes) and redistributed them to people in need of housing. U.S. owned casinos and houses of prostitution (so many in fact that Cuba was referred to as 'the whore house of the Caribbean) were closed.

Che would go on to become President of the National Bank of Cuba and Minister of Industries, positions from which he headed the major challenge of transforming Cuba's backwards, colonial, capitalist plantation economy into a socialist industrialized economy. The U.S. government, angry that the socialist revolution had taken up the cause of the people over the interests of foreign-owned business, drastically cut back the amount of sugar that they purchased from Cuba (eventually imposing a full economic embargo, which stands to this day, even though it has been repeatedly condemned by all but 2 nations and deemed illegal by the United Nations), in an attempt to damage the Cuban economy. They also sabotaged buildings, farms, and factories, flew planes over the island dropping bombs, and attempted to assassinate Cuban leaders. Cuba however, would not be intimidated. Che negotiated a trade agreement with the Soviet Union in 1960 in which they agreed to buy all Cuban sugar at a price above the going rate. He also represented Cuba on many trade missions to nations in Europe, Africa, and Asia.

Che played a major part in the reorganization of the Cuban economy along a socialist path, which enabled the country to eliminate homelessness, illiteracy, and unemployment in only a few years. He became well known as a hero of many for his fiery attacks on the United States imperialists' foreign policy in Africa, Asia, and Latin America.

It was during this time that Che made many important theoretical contributions in his speeches, articles, letters, and essays. His book *Guerrilla Warfare* became highly influential, and was used as a guide by guerrilla movements throughout Latin America (unfortunately, many of the fighters, though very courageous, oversimplified the theories put forth in the book, eventually leading to their defeat). Groups like the FARC-EP, waging a decades long revolutionary struggle in Colombia, utilize many methods laid out in the book to this day. *Man and Socialism in Cuba*, put forth many of Che, and Cuba's, greatest contributions. In it Che pointed out that liberation of humankind could only come about after the people first evolved into 'new people', concerned with the welfare of everyone as a whole over the welfare of themselves as individuals. This 'evolution' could only occur when the material conditions for it existed, namely, under socialism. Later, when the continuing world revolution, and the economic crises inherent to capitalism destabilized it, the need for the proletarian state would disappear and full liberation would finally exist in a society of equals without states or governments.

Che portrayed this 'new man' in his daily life. He spent

his weekends and evenings volunteering in shipyards and textile factories or cutting sugarcane. He was known for his simple lifestyle, an example of which was when he refused a pay raise when he became a member of government, choosing instead to continue receiving the much lower salary he drew as a *Comandante* in the Rebel Army. In another famous example, when Che was served food on expensive china while dining with high-ranking officials from the Communist Party of the Soviet Union during a trip to Russia, he asked the officials, "Is this how the working class lives in Russia?"

An attempted U.S. invasion, commonly known as 'the Bay of Pigs', and which was defeated in less than 72 hours, took place during Che's time in the revolutionary government. The event lead Cuba to acquire nuclear missiles from the USSR in its own defense, which resulted in the "Cuban missile crisis" in 1962.

The Disappearance

After returning from a three-month tour of the People's Republic of China, United Arab Republic, Algeria, Ghana, Mali, Dahomey, Congo-Brazzaville, and Tanzania in March of 1965, Che dropped out of public life and was not seen for some time.

Che's whereabouts were the main question in Cuba throughout the year, and many rumors began to spread – including one started by enemies of the revolution that Che and Fidel had some sort of a split. This of course was not true at all, as would be proven later.

In an interview with foreign correspondents on November 1st, Castro said that he knew where Guevara was but could not disclose the location. He said that Che was "in the best of health". Speculation however continued at the end of the year, and Che's movements would have to be kept secret for the next two years.

During this time, an article written by Che was

published in *Tricontinental Magazine* in which he called for complete support of the heroic Vietnamese people who were fighting against U.S. imperialist invaders, and urged comrades around the world to create "two, three, many Vietnams."

In The Congo

In March of 1965 the decision was made that Che would lead a rebel force in support of the Marxist Simba movement in the former Belgian Congo (later Zaire and currently the Democratic Republic of the Congo) in Africa.

Guevara worked with guerrilla leader Laurent-Desire Kabila, who had earlier helped supporters of the murdered prime minister Patrice Lumumba lead a revolt that was suppressed by the Congolese army and a large group of white mercenaries.

CIA advisors working with the Congolese army monitored Guevara's communications, arranged ambushes against the rebels and the Cubans, and interrupted their supply lines. Che had planned to teach the local Simba fighters communist ideology and the strategies and tactics of guerrilla warfare; but, due to their incompetence, superstition, and internal feuds, he was unable to, and the revolt eventually failed. After seven months, Che, who was ill and suffering from debilitating bouts of asthma, finally left the Congo with the surviving members of his Cuban column (six had died in battle). Originally, Che refused to give up and planned to send the wounded back to Cuba and then stand alone, fighting to the end as a revolutionary example; but after much debating with his comrades in arms, and Fidel, he was finally persuaded to return. Guevara documented his experiences in his *Congo Diaries* (later published as *The African Dream*).

During his time in the Congo, Fidel had made public a farewell letter written to him in which Che officially severed his ties with Cuba in order to devote himself to revolutionary activities in other parts of the world. "I feel that I have fulfilled the part of my duty that tied me to the Cuban revolution in its territory," the letter says, "And I say goodbye to you, the comrades, your people, who are already mine … Other nations of the world call for my modest efforts. I can do that which is denied you because of your responsibility as the head of Cuba, and the time has come for us to part."

After spending six months living underground in Dar-es-Salaam, Prague, and the German Democratic Republic, Che returned to Cuba, but only on a temporary basis for the few months needed to prepare another revolutionary effort, this time in Latin America.

Throughout 1966 and 1967 people continued to wonder where exactly Che was. Finally, in a speech at the 1967 May Day rally in Havana, Major Juan Almeida announced that Guevara was "serving the revolution somewhere in Latin America." It would turn out that Che was leading a guerrilla army in Bolivia.

Che chose Bolivia after a 1964 coup triggered an outbreak in demonstrations, protests, strike by miners, and repression against leaders of leftist and other popular movements. When he and his comrades analyzed the situation, they saw that there was an opening for a guerrilla column made up of Bolivians, some Peruvians, and a group of well trained Cubans, to launch a revolutionary offensive. The plan was to create an international rebel army, that, after achieving victory in Bolivia, would spread the struggle to the rest of Latin America.

A piece of land was purchased in the jungles of the Nancahuazu by the Bolivian Communist party and turned over to Che for use as a training area. The Party originally pledged its full support and participation of its membership, but its leader, Mario Monjae, later decided against it after the struggle had already begun.

The rebel army, named the *Ejercito de Liberacion Nacional de Bolivia* (National Liberation Army of Bolivia), was made up of about 50 well equipped guerrillas. They were able to launch a number of successful attacks against the Bolivian army in the mountainous Camiri region, despite the fact that it was being trained in jungle warfare and aided by U.S. Army Special Forces.

But problems, such as the refusal of the Communist Party of Bolivia to deliver expected assistance, materials, and reinforcements (the Party leadership went as far as to refuse to tell would-be volunteers how and where to join the guerrillas), eventually lead to some defeats. In September the Bolivian Army managed to eliminate two small groups of guerrillas.

Additionally, counter-revolutionary Cuban exiles with full CIA backing set up interrogation houses in which they tortured 300,000 Bolivians in search of supporters of Che and the guerrillas.

Capture and Assassination

To make matters worse a deserter betrayed the guerrillas and lead Bolivian Special Forces directly to them. On October 8th, their encampment was encircled and a shoot out took place. Che refused to surrender and was captured only after being shot in both knees and having his gun destroyed by a bullet.

Che was taken to a old schoolhouse where he was held overnight. On the next afternoon he was murdered by a sergeant in the Bolivian army while he was tied by his hands to a board. Before he was executed, Che said these last words: "I know you are here to kill me. Shoot coward! You are only going to kill a man."

After a military doctor cut off Che's hands, Bolivian army officers moved his body to an undisclosed location and refused to reveal if his remains had been buried or cremated.

CIA agent Felix Rodriguez, who also took part in the

failed invasions of Cuba and Vietnam, took Che's watch and still displays it to this day.

On October 15 Fidel Castro gave an emotional speech in which informed the world of Che's death and proclaimed three days of public mourning in Cuba. The death was considered a severe blow to the revolutionary movement and deeply saddened oppressed people around the world.

The diary Che kept in Bolivia was removed when he was captured. In it, he documented the events of the guerrilla campaign. He wrote of how the guerrillas were forced to begin operation much earlier than they had planned due to discovery by the Bolivian Army. He also recorded the rift between the Bolivian Communist Party and himself, which resulted in the rebel army having far fewer soldiers and contacts than was originally expected. Che also wrote of his increasing illness towards the end of the campaign. His asthma was getting worse, and most of his last offensives were made simply to obtain medicine.

In 1997, Che's skeletal remains were exhumed from beneath an air strip near Vallegrande, Bolivia, positively identified by DNA matching, and returned to Cuba. On October 17, 1997, his remains were laid to rest with full military honors in a specially built mausoleum, the *Plaza Comandante Ernesto Guevara*, in the city of Santa Clara, where he won the decisive battle of the Cuban Revolution thirty-nine years earlier.

Legacy of a Revolutionary Hero

When Che's murder was announced protests broke out throughout the world, and articles, books, poems and songs were written about his life, death, and message. Che is especially revered because of his spirit of self-sacrifice, illustrated by his choice to reject a comfortable life and instead join, and take up the cause of the worlds poor, oppressed majority. He never gave up that cause, continuing to give his all to the revolutionary struggle until his death.

The famous photo taken of Che by photographer Alberto Korda in 1960, which became one of the 20th centuries most recognizable images, has become a symbol of liberation for millions of people.

French philosopher Jean-Paul Sarte called Che "the most complete human being of our age." Ernesto "Che" Guevara was one of the most dedicated revolutionaries we have ever known. But his struggle is far from over. The oppressed masses of the world must continue to fight for freedom, justice, and equality through socialist revolution – the only way it can be achieved – as Che said, *"Hasta la victoria, siempre!"* [Forever, until victory!]

Hurricane Katrina and Capitalism: A Disaster in the Making

On August 29, 2005, Katrina, one of the most powerful hurricanes in history, slammed into the coast of the South Eastern United States, washing away entire towns in Mississippi and destroying much of New Orleans.

No one knows how many people have died in this disaster, but estimates range from hundreds to even thousands, and up to one million have been left homeless.

The toxic water, which is flooding the streets of New Orleans, is a mixture of garbage, raw sewage, gasoline and other petroleum products from nearby oil refineries, thousands of corpses--of those who died in the hurricane as well as those washed out of the cemeteries, and poisonous chemicals from the many chemical plants in the region (more per square mile than in any other region in the U.S.). The effects of this will likely be felt by the people and environment of the area for years to come.

Tens, possibly hundreds of thousands are stranded on rooftops and in attacks. The "relief" effort has proven to be too little, too late. "We are out here like pure animals," cried a survivor, "We don't have help."

In response to the increasingly desperate survivors' appropriations of food and water, the government has proclaimed *de facto* martial law, with soldiers and police enforcing a "shoot to kill" policy. The entire area has descended into chaos.

Although hurricanes cannot be prevented, catastrophic results like these can.

Cuba, a socialist country which is organized to meet human needs, has shown that it's possible to carry out large scale evacuations with very little resources. Less then two months ago, 1.7 million people were evacuated on short notice in preparation for Hurricane Dennis.

In Cuba, both the pickup and delivery of people for evacuations is organized well in advance. The population is well educated about hurricanes, and they know where to go (and how to get there) in emergency situations.

The country's leaders and knowledgeable meteorologists take charge, going on television and keeping the population informed. In case of power outages, there are special messengers who communicate evacuation plans to each area.

People go door to door to inform everyone of upcoming evacuations, and return to let them know when they have begun.

All shelters are staffed with medical personnel and family doctors evacuate along with their neighborhoods, knowing who needs special medicines (such as diabetics and asthmatics) and bringing them along in sufficient quantities. Veterinarians evacuate animals and items such as televisions and refrigerators are brought along so that people don't stay behind in attempts to protect them.

If all else fails, people can be evacuated to high schools in the countryside which contain built-in dormitories.

Because of measures like these, made possible by Cuba's social revolution, the last category 4 hurricane to hit Cuba left only 16 dead – the highest death toll in forty-one years(!) in an island constantly bombarded by hurricanes.

But in the U.S., a capitalist country where profit rules over people, evacuations like these are not only not planned for, they are in fact blocked!

Airlines stopped flights to New Orleans twenty-four hours before they had to, only because it wouldn't have been *profitable* to fly airplanes with no passengers on them.

Commercial buses have lined up on Interstate 10 of the

city, refusing to evacuate people with no money. "It's like they're punishing us," said one 52-year-old survivor.

The U.S. government, which has spent hundreds of billions of dollars on a war based on lies, didn't spend a single penny evacuating a city directly in the path of one of the worst hurricanes in history – even though they knew it was coming days in advance!

The levees, built to protect the city from disasters like this one, were not maintained before the hurricane hit and couldn't hold up to the impact of the water and wind. As a direct result of the funding of the Iraq war and Bush's tax cuts for the wealthy, many U.S. Army Corps of Engineers requests for hurricane protection projects have been cut back or delayed since 2001.

As the *Chicago Tribune* reported, "Despite continuous warnings that a catastrophic hurricane could hit New Orleans, the Bush administration and Congress in recent years have repeatedly cut funding for hurricane preparation and flood control. The cuts have delayed construction of levees around the city and stymied an ambitious project to improve drainage in New Orleans' neighborhoods."

At least nine articles in the *Times-Picayune* from 2004 and 2005 specifically cite the cost of Iraq as a reason for the lack of hurricane and flood-control dollars.

The corporate controlled media has portrayed victims of the hurricane, who are struggling to survive, as "looters" and "miscreants." The media coverage has also revealed the deep rooted racism that prevails in this society – White survivors are portrayed as 'refugees' who 'find' food and other supplies while Blacks are demonized and depicted as savage criminals. The results of slavery, Jim Crow segregation laws, and the ongoing oppression of Blacks and other minorities has been brought to the front.

The truth is, these survivors are taking food, water, dry

clothing, and other items because they need them survive -- they have been abandoned and have no other choice!

So what *has* been the response of the government?

Louisiana's governor has called for a day of prayer when she should have been working to meet the needs of the hurricanes victims!

Federal Emergency Management Director Michael Brown went as far as placing the blame on the victims themselves, saying "I think the death toll may go into the thousands and that's going to be attributable a lot to people who did not heed the advance warnings [to leave]."

The reality of the situation is that the over 100,000 people that remained in New Orleans and the surrounding areas hit by the hurricane didn't have the financial means to leave! As a survivor told reporters, "that's a crime, and people are angry about it!"

People are angry, and for good reason. But instead of attempting to relieve their anger by doing what should have been done in the first place, the emphasis of the government is being placed on stopping the "looting" and "lawlessness" of the hurricane victims!

President Bush, taking a break from his long vacation, urged a "crackdown," saying "I think there ought to be zero tolerance of people breaking the law, and I've made that clear to our attorney general."

Thousands of troops, "fresh back from Iraq," have been sent to New Orleans and thousands more are on the way. "These are some of the 40,000 extra troops that I have demanded," said Louisiana's governor (the same person who called for a day of prayer), as she went on to threaten the hurricane victims, "They have M-16s, and they're locked and loaded ... I have one message for these hoodlums: These troops know how to shoot and kill, and they are more than willing to do so if necessary, and I expect they will."

U.S. Coast Guard rescue missions have been suspended, and boat rescue teams looking for Katrina survivors have been ordered to stand down by the Federal Emergency Management Agency.

New Orleans Mayor Nagin ordered the police force to abandon search-and-rescue efforts and focus on stopping the "criminals."

Police officers armed with shotguns are standing outside of hotels to keep out refugees looking for food, water, and shelter, while snipers are stationed on police station rooftops to "protect" private property. Officers attempted to keep camera crews from filming their actions under the pretense that the streets were "too dangerous."

Police from Texas, Arkansas, Kentucky, and as far away as Michigan are being called in to "bring order back to the streets." Of course, no one was called in to help with evacuation or relief efforts earlier.

This disaster, and the government's response to it, have shown unequivocally that the people of New Orleans and the other areas hit by Hurricane Katrina are not only victims of a natural disaster, they are victims of the capitalist system – a ruthless system based on the exploitation of the majority of humanity for the benefit of the few, in which private property and profit are considered more important than human life.

This did not have to happen this way, and it doesn't have to ever happen again! A much better world for all of us *is possible*! Now, more than ever, we must push onward to a socialist revolution to liberate all of humanity!

The Catastrophe in Haiti: The crisis that capitalism created

By now, news of the immense disaster in Haiti has reached every corner of earth. On Tuesday, January 12, 2010, a massive magnitude 7.0 Mw earthquake occurred, reeking widespread devastation in the southern part of the country. After the dust cleared, some 200,000 people were dead with another 1,200,000 left homeless. Weeks later, untold numbers of people are clamoring for food, water and shelter.

But the social catastrophe in Haiti has much more to do with the social system dominant in the world today than geology.

The Caribbean island of Hispaniola is home to both the Dominican Republic and Haiti. African slaves were brought to the island, which was originally known as *Kiskeya*, by Spanish and French colonizers after the native Taínos were killed off by a combination of forced labor, murder and exotic disease. For decades, these slaves labored on plantations under detestable conditions, subject to murder and worse.

One former slave described life under the French colonizers in detail: "Have they not hung up men with heads downward, drowned them in sacks, crucified them on planks, buried them alive, crushed them in mortars? Have they not forced them to eat excrement? And, having flayed them with the lash, have they not cast them alive to be devoured by worms, or onto anthills, or lashed them to stakes in the swamp to be devoured by mosquitoes? Have they not thrown them into boiling cauldrons of cane syrup? Have they not put men and women inside barrels studded with spikes and rolled them down mountainsides into the abyss? Have they not consigned these miserable blacks to man-eating dogs until the latter, sated by human flesh, left the mangled victims to be finished off with bayonet and poniard?"

A large of number of slaves risked their lives to escape the madness, surviving in the mountains and launching occasional raids on French plantations. This state of things lasted into the late 18th Century, when a slave rebellion broke out in the years immediately following the French Revolution. After years of intense struggle on the part of the enslaved majority, the country of Haiti was born in 1804.

The first independent state founded by former African slaves, and the second republic ever established in the Western Hemisphere, Haiti has been subject to a never ending imperialist onslaught from its earliest days.

The leaders of the United States were unable to tolerate Haiti's independence, as its very existence endangered the slave economy of the southern states. The U.S. aided French attempts to retake the Haiti, imposed an economic embargo on the country, and refused to recognize its independence for close to sixty years.

The imperialist powers of France, Britain and Spain were no more willing to accept the existence of the fledgling country. All three cut off trade with Haiti in an attempt to ruin its economy. Recognition from the French came only after Haitian leaders agreed to pay huge sums for money for compensation of French-owned lands lost in the rebellion. Unable to come up with the necessary funds, the new country had to take out loans from France, forcing it into a state of debt.

Subsequently, Haiti was forced even further into debt, causing it to take out loans from Wall Street.

Still, France continued to dominate its former colony economically and politically until 1915, when the United States Marines invaded Haiti to collect outstanding loans granted by U.S. banks. The U.S. forces did not leave the country until 1934.

Under the stewardship of the Marines, Haiti was reorganized to serve the interests of U.S. capitalists.

In 1956, François 'Papa Doc' Duvalier rose to become president of Haiti with U.S. support. A brutal dictator with a notorious death squad that grew to be twice as large as the country's military, Duvalier received Washington's backing on the grounds that he served as a bulwark against "communism."

Duvalier kept his grip on Haiti until his death in 1971, when his son Jean-Claude "Baby Doc" Duvalier took power at age 19. The U.S. continued its support for the Duvalier dynasty. In 1984, Ernest Preeg, the U.S. ambassador to Haiti lauded Jean-Claude's rule as "the longest period of violence-free stability in the nation's history." Unfortunately, the countless people murdered during this time were unable to object to this statement. After years of continuing in his father's bloody footsteps, "Baby Doc" was finally overthrown in a popular uprising in 1986. He fled Haiti in an American Air Force plane.

The following years were dominated by military coups, popular uprisings and more U.S. invasions. Loans from international imperialist banking outfits like the International Monetary Fund (IMF) were extended to Haiti under the condition that the country's economy and labor force be opened wide to "free trade" exploitation.

The left populist Jean-Bertrand Aristide was elected with the mass support of the urban poor in 1990. A year later he was overthrown in a military coup.

Eschewing his earlier promises to be independent of Washington, Aristide begged the U.S. to help him retake power. After receiving promises from Aristide to sell off national property to foreign capitalists, U.S. President Bill Clinton sent 20,000 U.S. soldiers to Haiti to reinstall Aristide in 1994.

But he did not bend far enough. In 2004, during his second term as President, Aristide was overthrown in a military coup backed by the U.S., France and Canada and forced out of the country. United States President George W. Bush sent troops to once again occupy Haiti until a United Nations occupation force made up of mercenary military forces from various parts of Latin America was established.

The combined effects of that (ongoing) occupation, previous invasions and occupations, embargos, corrupt imperialist-backed dictatorships, years of economic and political servitude, and "free trade reforms" led directly to Haiti's current condition. Haiti is the poorest country in the Western Hemisphere. Upwards of 80 percent of people in Haiti live in abject poverty, surviving on less than $2 a day. A mere 53 percent of the population can read and write and one quarter of the country's Gross Domestic Product comes from remittances of Haitians living abroad.

The imperialist-capitalist earthquake that has been ravaging Haiti for hundreds of years set the stage for the mass devastation and human suffering that has resulted from the January 2010 earthquake.

The inability to compete with U.S.-based agricultural corporations subsidized by Washington has driven countless small farmers to the Haitian capital of Port-au-Prince over the years. Unable to find work in the city, these farmers and their families have taken up residence in shacks thrown together in sprawling shanty towns like Cité Soleil.

Unlike imperialist countries such as Japan, where the latest technology is used to create earthquake proof buildings, construction in Haiti is often done with whatever materials are available. Steel rebar, which is necessary to reinforce concrete, is absent from many buildings and virtually all shacks. Unable to afford the necessary amount of concrete, many builders also forgo the laying of a basic foundation on which to build. Years of "brain drain" –that is, the flight of educated people with technical knowhow, such as architects and engineers, to the imperialist centers where the pay is much higher—only compounds these problems.

The military invasion of Haiti ordered by U.S. President Barrack Obama in the immediate aftermath of the earthquake has caused even further calamity.

In a clear attempt to repaint U.S. imperialism as a "humanitarian force," the capitalist ruling class and its media have stepped up the propaganda in a major way to promote Washington's supposedly benevolent response to the earthquake.

But there's nothing humanitarian about this mission. The first ships sent to Haiti were of a purely military nature. The sole hospital ship sent by the U.S. arrived over a week after the guided missile cruiser, nuclear-powered aircraft carrier, etc. And neither the ships nor the numerous military planes that landed in Haiti carried supplies meant for the victims of the earthquake.

By all accounts, the U.S. forces in Haiti have actually been interfering in the distribution of aid. Supply planes have been turned back, volunteers have been rerouted and crucial aid has been delayed.

A spokesperson for the volunteer organization Doctors Without Borders explained to the Reuters news agency that "planes carrying urgently needed surgical equipment and drugs have been turned away five times, even though the agency received prior authorization to land."

What about all that aid Obama pledged for Haiti? A recent report by the Associated Press showed that 30 cents of every dollar of that "aid" is going to the U.S. military forces occupying the country! A mere 10 cents of each dollar is going toward the purchase of food while a measly penny of each dollar is going to the Haitian government for reconstruction.

One can expect much of the same from the much-lauded "Clinton Bush Haiti Fund" – ludicrously named after two U.S. Presidents that ordered invasions of Haiti—launched by Obama. Perhaps this is why former president George W. Bush said "I know a lot of people want to send blankets or water [but] just send your cash."

With the Haitian state in shambles and the imperialist-backed government rendered impotent, the U.S. has decided to take direct control of Haiti rather than let it fall into the hands of the Haitian people themselves. As added bonuses, the U.S. rulers hope to deflect criticism of their ongoing occupations of Afghanistan and Iraq, drum up support for their increasing operations in countries like Pakistan and Yemen, and give their soldiers vital experience in quelling unrest for possible use at home as the economic crisis continues to expand.

The imperialists have consistently proven that they have nothing to offer Haiti besides exploitation and increasing misery. What exists of a local ruling class has proven itself to be totally subservient to the imperialists.

Haiti can only move forward when the working class there stands up and organizes independent action. The Haitian working class must lead a struggle to drive the imperialist forces and their servants out of their country once and for all. They must organize themselves to carry out the aid and relief work they require. Such organization can create a framework on which a new, workers republic can be built.

It is the duty of workers elsewhere in the world to stand with their sisters and brothers in Haiti and offer as much concrete assistance as possible. In the United States specifically, this means that workers must fight for the immediate withdraw of all U.S. forces from Haiti.

As the crisis in Haiti has again illustrated, two choices lay before us: a continuing slide into barbarism or a working class revolution to drive out the rulers and reorganize society to meet human need.

The Soweto Uprising: When Young South Africans Shook the World

June 16 [2006] marks the 30th anniversary of the Soweto uprising in South Africa. The uprising was a very important event during which the youths of South Africa -- fed up with decades of injustice -- dealt a fatal blow to the racist apartheid system from which it would never be able to recover.

Background

Apartheid (which literally means "apartness" in Dutch) was the system of racial segregation under which South Africa was ruled by white Afrikaaner settlers from 1948 on. A legacy of European colonialism, it was a racist system in which the white capitalist minority maintained their rule. Under apartheid, people were classified into racial groups -- White, Black, Indian and Coloured (by law, these terms were capitalized) -- and were forcibly separated from each other on the basis of this classification.

The Black majority were named citizens of "homelands" (to which a majority never belonged), which were like reservations for Native Americans in the U.S.. This prevented them from being able to vote or participate in any meaningful way in South African society.

Black South Africans received poor medical care and educations (if they could afford them at all!), while the hospitals and schools available to whites were of superior quality. On top of this, Black workers received much lower pay than workers classified as white.

Blacks weren't allowed to travel to "white areas" (the majority of the country) unless they had a pass (which were only issued for work). Sixty-nine unarmed Blacks were shot dead by police in Sharpeville during a peaceful protest against these "pass laws" in 1960.

Blacks weren't allowed to use facilities (libraries, beaches, pools, cinemas, parks, ambulances, restaurants, graveyards, bridges, bathrooms, churches, hotels, etc.) or transportation designated for "whites only" either. There were few facilities (especially libraries, parks and pools) designated for use by Blacks at all. Sex or marriage out of one's designated race was also strictly prohibited.

Under apartheid, the South African Communist Party, African National Congress or ANC (at the time an anti-apartheid group, but now a bourgeois political party, to which Nelson Mandela has belonged for over six decades), and the Pan Africanist Congress (a Black nationalist party) were all banned, and trade unions for Blacks and "coloureds" (mixed race) weren't recognized until the 1980's.

A state-of-emergency was declared in the 1960's which allowed the police and military to detain Blacks without trial. Some 18,000 Blacks were arrested in the 1960's, including Nelson Mandela, who was sentenced to life in prison on charges of "terrorism" for his role in the fight against apartheid.

The apartheid system was condemned by many countries around the world and was opposed by about 20 percent of South Africa's white population. On November 6, 1962, the United Nations General Assembly passed Resolution 1761, condemning South African apartheid. In 1973, the General Assembly agreed upon something called the International Convention on the Suppression and Punishment of the Crime of Apartheid, which was intended to provide a legal basis with which member states could apply sanctions against South Africa to pressure its government to end apartheid. Notably, the imperialist U.S. government was one of the few countries to remain close to the South African apartheid government almost until the end of its existence, even going as far as supporting their labeling of the ANC as a terrorist organization.

U.S. President Ronald Reagan took it just a step farther, calling the ANC "a notorious terrorist organization", while justifying his support of the South African regime by saying it was "a country that has stood by us in every war we've ever fought, a country that, strategically, is essential to the free world in its production of minerals."

In 1974, despite protests from The African Teachers Association, a law was passed by the apartheid government called the "Afrikaans Medium Decree" which forced all black students to learn the Afrikaans language and to be taught all school subjects in it. Of course, white students could still be taught in the language of their choice.

Black South Africans fervently opposed the law, and students immediately protested being forced to speak the language of the oppressor.

Illustrating the dictatorial rule of the apartheid government, Paul Janson, who was then the Deputy Minister of Bantu Education, boldly stated: "No, I have not consulted the African people on the language issue and I'm not going to."

At the same time, the apartheid government tried somewhat to justify the new law by saying that since the apartheid government "paid for education for Blacks", they had the right to decide on the language of instruction. This was pure fiction. In fact, under apartheid, only white schools were fully subsidized, which meant that only whites could attend school for free. Black South Africans had to pay R102 (a months wages for an average worker at the time) to send two children to school for a year. They also had to buy textbooks, which were free for white students, and had to contribute towards the cost of constructing schools.

The Last Straw

Anger and protests increased dramatically in February, 1976, after two teachers were fired in for refusing to teach Afrikaans.

In response to growing popular opposition to the Afrikaans Medium Decree, one white official in the apartheid government said: "If students are not happy, they should stay away from school since attendance is not compulsory for Africans."

Disgust among Black South Africans towards the law continued to grow, culminating on April 30, 1976, when students at Orlando West Junior School in Soweto went on strike, refusing to attend school. The strike soon spread to many other schools in Soweto, and a group called the Soweto Students' Representative Council – made up of representatives of students from each of Soweto's schools – organized a demonstration to take place on June 16, to make the voices of Black students heard.

The students planned for the demonstration in secret, surprising the apartheid government – and even their own parents – with their display of strength when June 16, 1976 came along.

The uprising

On the morning of June 16, thousands of students came together, as was planned, and staged a major rally against the Afrikaans Medium Decree and the racist apartheid system that gave birth to it. The demonstration grew as the morning went on, with many students who found out about it just that morning joining in, instead of going to school.

The students planned to march peacefully from Naledi and Morris Isaacson High Schools to Orlando Stadium, with other students and supporters joining in along the way. Their effort was enthusiastically supported by Soweto teachers and Soweto's Black population in general.

As the students began to march, they came to find that the police had blocked their route to Orlando Stadium with barricades. Even with this provocation by the fascist apartheid forces, the students remained restrained and continued on an alternative route. The apartheid police then called in reinforcements.

At this point there were tens of thousand of students marching, many holding up placards with slogans such as "Down with Afrikaans, Viva Azania" (Azania was the name used by nationalists for South Africa), and "If we must do Afrikaans, Vorster must do Zulu" (Vorster was the white Prime Minister of South Africa at the time, and Zulu is the native language of many Black South Africans).

The racist police became frustrated with their inability to deter the students and resorted to brute force. First they released vicious dogs, then they shot cans of tear gas into the crowd of Black students. When the students responded by throwing rocks, the fascist police opened fire on them, killing 5 students immediately and causing mayhem as thousands of students ran in panic.

A photograph of the lifeless body of one of the first victims, 13-year-old Hector Pieterson (pictured left), being carried away by another student with blood dripping from his mouth, became a symbol of the brutality of the racist apartheid regime and their fascist police enforcers.

The shootings sparked a mass uprising of young Black South Africans tired of the unjust apartheid system. Young men and women, armed with little more than rocks and pieces of trash, battled the apartheid police in the streets, and, in an offensive against the apartheid state, burned government buildings, government-owned liquor stores, and the cars of government officials.

"Soweto was on fire," Peter Magubane, a photographer who lived in Soweto at the time, later said of the uprising. "The children were angry. Ten-year-olds were in the streets picking up stones and throwing. Where there was anything burning, you would find these 10-year-olds, 9-year-olds, saying 'Power, Power!' You realized that the political mood had changed."

In response, the apartheid government sent in the army, who joined with police in firing their guns randomly at Black youths in the area. Local emergency clinics were full of young Black children with gun shot wounds, many of whom could not be saved. By days end, hundreds of children had been killed. But even this wasn't enough to squash the popular resistance. Within days, the uprising had spread to Pretoria, Durban, Transvaal and Orange Free State.

The violent response of the apartheid police to the students peaceful protest against the Afrikaans Medium Decree set off a nationwide revolt. The oppressed Black masses of South Africa had had enough of racism, segregation, exploitation, repression and police brutality. They had had enough of apartheid.

After four months, Black South Africans in some 160 communities across the country had joined in the mass revolt. Some protested peacefully while others actively attacked the apartheid government and its enforcers. The apartheid government responded with more violent repression, and, in an attempt to leave the rest of South Africa and the world in the dark, also banned journalists from entering the townships where rebellions occurred.

A growing number of white South African workers and students opposed the apartheid government's actions as well. Hundreds of white students from the University of Witwatersrand marched in Johannesburg to protest the killing of children by the racist police. As their campaign progressed, they joined with striking Black workers in opposing the apartheid regime.

On the first anniversary of the police attack on the Soweto students, as the revolt it sparked was still going on, the ANC successfully called a strike against the apartheid system.

The ongoing clashes between students, workers and farmers and the police and army, as well as strikes, caused a serious economic crisis in South Africa which lead to a drastic devaluation of South African currency and shook the foundations of the white capitalists' apartheid system.

The rebellion the Soweto Uprising set off – which sounded the death knell for apartheid – would continue until the end of 1977.

Aftermath

The photo of Hector Pieterson's lifeless body got the world's attention. Millions across the globe stood in solidarity with South Africa's oppressed Black majority, and many got involved in the struggle for majority rule there. Especially instrumental was socialist Cuba, whose selfless internationalist aid to then-recently-independent Angola (when it was invaded by South Africa's army in 1975) contributed greatly to the downfall of apartheid.

The Soweto Uprising awakened many Black South Africans, who joined actively in the resistance against apartheid, as well as a number of whites, who subsequently withdrew their support for the racist system.

Although the apartheid government continued their violent repression, they couldn't maintain their rule over South Africa. Growing popular revolts and opposition, the defeat of the South African army in Angola, sabotage, and a guerrilla war lead by the armed wing of the ANC lead to the downfall of apartheid between 1990 and 1994.

In honor of the young Black South Africans who shook the world 30 years ago, June 16 is now celebrated in South

Africa as "Youth Day".

The Struggle Continues

To be sure, vast inequality and the exploitation of man by man – that is capitalism – still exist in South Africa; but the overthrow of apartheid was definitely progressive and something we revolutionaries completely supported.

The fight for freedom, justice and equality for all – that is, the fight for socialism – by the multi-racial working class majority against the ruling capitalist minority in South Africa continues today, inspired by the example of the heroic Black South African majority, who united in struggle to end the rule of the privileged white minority.

Hail the Vietnamese Victory Over US Imperialism!

Celebrate the 30th Anniversary of the victory of the heroic Vietnamese People!

Saturday, April 30, 2005, marked the 30th anniversary of the fall of Saigon, which signified the victory of the heroic Vietnamese people's struggle against imperialism after many years of war.

Cuban Defense Minister Raul Castro began a week-long visit to Vietnam on Tuesday, April 26th, where he will join tens of thousands of it's people in celebrations of the anniversary. He is accompanied by Cuban Foreign Minister Felipe Perez Roque, Ramiro Valdes (an original military commander of the July 26th movement that lead the victorious Cuban Revolution), and Fernando Remirez de Estenoz, head of international relations for the Communist Party of Cuba. Cuban leaders such as Fidel Castro and Ernesto 'Che' Guevara were among the most vocal in calling for increased support to the Vietnamese people from the so-called 'socialist bloc' during the war.

It was on April 30th, in 1975, that a North Vietnamese (People's Army of Vietnam) tank crashed through the gates of the presidential palace in Saigon, long since renamed Ho Chi Minh city after the revolutionary leader and founder of the Vietnamese Communist Party.

The Vietnam War, in which the US military utilized terrorism and napalm against combatants and civilians alike in an attempt to crush the will of the Vietnamese people in their struggle for national liberation, and which left 58,000 US troops and nearly 4,000,000 Vietnamese men, women and children dead, ended a few hours after the departure of the last

Americans by helicopter from the roof of the US embassy. The puppet president of the Republic of Vietnam (South Vietnam), General Duong Van Minh (aka Big Minh) -- who had been hastily installed in the regime's dying days -- had no choice but to admit defeat. The National Liberation Front's blue and red flag with a golden star was raised above the palace.

Unfortunately, and to a large extent because of the material conditions of the time, the Vietnamese people weren't able to establish socialism even after victory, contrary to claims of the Communist Party of Vietnam. The Free People's movement stands in solidarity with the people of Vietnam; and while recognizing their achievements, and supporting them against imperialism, we must also be critical of the Vietnamese government's policies and push for increased worker control and worker's democracy so that socialism can finally be realized.

Nonetheless April 30 marks a historic day in the struggle of oppressed people around the world. Let us celebrate this monumental achievement, knowing a defeat of imperialism anywhere is a victory for oppressed people everywhere!

Documents reveal pretense for U.S. invasion of Vietnam was a lie

Something that many around the world have known for decades has been verified by recently declassified documents; the second attack on U.S. ships in the Gulf of Tonkin -- the main rationale used by the U.S. for the invasion of Vietnam -- never happened!

Claims that North Vietnamese boats attacked two U.S. warships on August 4, 1964, were the basis of the "Gulf of Tonkin resolution" which passed congress three days later, empowering then President Lyndon B. Johnson to take "all necessary steps" in the region and opening the way for all out invasion.

At the time Robert McNamara, Johnson's Secretary of Defense, claimed that there was "unequivocal proof" of an "unprovoked" attack.

Daniel Ellsberg, who was on duty in the Pentagon the night of the so called "attack" receiving messages from the ship, later said that the U.S. ships were on a secret mission, codenamed DeSoto Patrols, inside of North Vietnamese territorial waters, to provoke the North Vietnamese.

In 1990, squadron commander James Stockdale, who was on of the U.S. pilots flying overhead August 4, stated that he "had the best seat in the house to watch that event, and our destroyers were just shooting at phantom targets — there were no PT boats there... There was nothing there but black water and American fire power."

Just as the U.S. government lied to gain support for their imperialist conquest of Iraq, lies were used to justify the war on Vietnam 40 years earlier.

Recent Developments

The National Security Agency released hundreds of documents on November 30 of this year in response to pressures from researchers trying to get to the bottom of what has become known as the "Gulf of Tonkin incident".

In October, 2005 the *New York Times* reported that historian Robert J. Hanyok had concluded that the NSA deliberately distorted intelligence reports regarding the August 4 incident. The historian's conclusions were originally published in the Winter 2000/Spring 2001 edition of the NSA's classified publication *Cryptologic Quarterly*. In it Mr. Hanyok declared that his review of the complete intelligence shows beyond a shadow of doubt that "no attack happened that night".

"In truth, Hanoi's navy was engaged in nothing that night but the salvage of two of the boats [that the U.S.] damaged on 2 August," he wrote.

In fact, he said that his analysis of previously top secret intelligence shows that the supposed attackers did not even know the location of the destroyers, the *USS Maddox* and *C. Turner Joy*, as the two ships patrolled off the North Vietnam coast.

"[T]he handful of SIGINT [signal intelligence --ed.] reports which suggested that an attack had occurred contained severe analytical errors, unexplained translation changes, and the conjunction of two unrelated messages into one translation," Hanyok said. "This latter product would become the Johnson administration's main proof of the August 4 attack."

According to intelligence officials, the U.S. government originally suppressed the release of the report because they didn't want comparisons to be made to the "intelligence" used to justify the invasion of Iraq in 2003.

"The parallels between the faulty intelligence on Tonkin Gulf and the manipulated intelligence used to justify the Iraq war make it all the more worthwhile to re-examine the events of

August 1964 in light of new evidence," said researcher John Prados, a specialist on the Gulf of Tonkin at George Washington University's National Security Archive.

Background
France colonized Indochina (Vietnam, Laos, and Cambodia) in the mid 1800's. Under this colonization Indochina became, for the most part, a giant plantation. The heroic Vietnamese people resisted this colonial rule all along. In 1930-31, the French suppressed a peasant uprising, killing 10,000 and deporting 50,000 more.

During World War II, Japan invaded Indochina, seizing administrative offices, banks, communications centers, and industries.

The Communist Lead Viet Minh, or "League for the Independence of Vietnam", which formed in 1941 to seek Vietnamese independence, began to fight against the Japanese.

The Viet Minh established revolutionary committees across the country, abolished forced labor (the corvée), began training local militia, and began returning to peasants the lands stolen from them by the French.

The U.S. used the independence fighters whenever they could. The Viet Minh frequently helped downed American pilots and U.S. military intelligence in the fight against the Japanese.

When Japan surrendered in August 1945, the Viet Minh, under the leadership of Ho Chi Minh, declared independence from France, forming the Democratic Republic of Vietnam on September 2, 1945.

But, with the Japanese beaten, the U.S. no longer had any "use" for the Viet Minh, and the French returned troops to Vietnam within a couple of months to reestablish their colonial rule. The Vietnamese people resisted fiercely.

The French, largely funded and politically supported by the United States, could not defeat the determined Vietnamese people. Finally, almost a decade later in 1954, the French surrendered after being badly beaten at the historic battle of Dien Bien Phu.

Shortly after, as a result of peace accords worked out in Geneva, Switzerland, all of Indochina was granted independence. Vietnam was temporarily divided into North and South Vietnam at the 17th Parallel until unifying elections could be held in 1956. The Viet Minh administrated North Vietnam as a socialist state, and Ho Chi Minh was named Prime Minister. The south was originally controlled by Emperor Bao Dai, but soon after the U.S. installed Ngo Dinh Diem as president. Over the next two years the government of South Vietnam would jail, torture, and execute at least 30,000 suspected communists.

South Vietnam and its chief supporter, the United States, reneged on the 1954 peace agreement and refused to hold unifying elections in 1956, realizing that Ho Chi Minh's widespread popularity would assure his victory.

In the words of U.S. President Eisenhower himself, "It was generally conceded that had an election been held, Ho Chi Minh would have been elected Premier." So much for "supporting democracy"!

The Vietnamese people were infuriated that the scheduled elections for the unification of the country never took place.

Soon after, a national front of all elements opposed to the U.S. puppet government in the government in the South formed the National Liberation Front (NLF) and initiated guerrilla activities.

The U.S. funded and supplied weapons to South Vietnam. U.S. military advisers, special forces, and finally regular troops were sent to help prop up the corrupt and unpopular government.

The U.S. government grew increasingly frustrated with Diem's inability to crush the popular rebellion taking place. After video footage of Buddhist monks lighting themselves on fire in protest of his repressive rule aired on televisions around the world, the U.S. sponsored a military coup which overthrew and killed Diem on November 1, 1963.

After the Gulf of Tonkin Resolution was passed in on August 7, 1964, (on the false pretenses stated above) the U.S. greatly increased its number of troops and attacks.

Over the next eleven years the U.S. would be responsible for one of the most brutal military campaigns in world history.

North Vietnam was continually carpet bombed, killing men, women, and children, and turning hospitals and schools into rubble. Napalm was dropped on villages, burning people alive, and the chemical weapon Agent Orange was dumped on farms and in water supplies -- still causing birth defects to this day. U.S. soldiers raped thousands of Vietnamese women and murdered countless innocent civilians. In one instance -- the My Lai Massacre -- 504 unarmed Vietnamese peasants, mostly old men, women, children, and babies were executed. Many were first tortured and/or raped. The U.S. army reported the event as a military victory resulting in the death of 128 enemy combatants.

Events like these were covered up all the time. Colin Powell, then a young US Army Major who was charged with investigating the massacre, wrote that "in direct refutation of this portrayal is the fact that relations between American soldiers and the Vietnamese people are excellent."

It wasn't until independent investigative journalist Seymour Hersh broke the My Lai story a year and a half later that the truth was finally revealed.

Comments made in a 1969 telephone conversation between U.S. National Security Advisor Henry Kissinger and

Secretary of Defense Melvin Laird, revealed recently by the National Security Archive, show that the photos of the war crime (published by *The Plain Dealer* in Cleveland, Ohio) were too shocking for senior officials to stage an effective cover-up. Laird is heard to say, "There are so many kids just lying there."

The Vietnamese were committed to resisting the foreign occupiers and struggling for their independence. They would not give up. The growing strength of the NLF, a huge anti-war movement, and the refusal by many U.S. soldiers to continue to take orders forced the U.S. began withdrawing its forces, though it continued to carry out deadly attacks.

Finally in the early hours of April 30, 1975, a People's Army of Vietnam tank crashed through the gates of the presidential palace in Saigon signaling the defeat of the U.S. backed regime and making way for the formation of the unified, Socialist Republic of Vietnam.

The U.S. invasion of Vietnam left nearly 4,000,000 Vietnamese men, women, and children, 300,000 Cambodian civilians, and 60,000 U.S. troops dead. Over 40,000 Vietnamese have been killed by landmines and unexploded ordnance since the war ended, and the environment and health continues to be effected by the chemical agents used by the U.S.

Stalingrad: When Communists Stopped the Nazi Monster

On February 2, 1943 the fascist German 6th Army surrendered to the Soviet Red Army after being defeated in what would go down in history as the bloodiest battle of all time.

Over 2,000,000 people (including at least 50,000 Soviet civilians) were killed in the months long battle. By the end, the population of Stalingrad – which was renamed Volgograd in 1961 as a part of Nikita Khruschev's "De-Stalinization" program – had fallen from 850,000 to just 1,500.

The Red Army's victory, which was made possible by the Soviet people's bravery and selfless sacrifice and the unbreakable spirit of socialism, dealt a decisive blow to the Nazis from which they were never able to recover.

Despite the fact that the official history of the West gives all the credit for the defeat of the fascist German-Italian-Japanese alliance to the U.S. and Britain, the truth is that the Soviet Union and other communist resistance armics did the bulk of the fighting and suffered the most loss of life and destruction.

Over 28,000,000 Soviets and 21,000,000 Chinese lost their lives in the fight against fascism, compared to 400,000 citizens of the U.S., and the Red Army engaged about 80% of all of Nazi Germany's forces throughout the war.

This isn't to say that the working people of the Western countries that fought in the war didn't make tremendous sacrifices, because they most certainly did, but we revolutionaries must be honest at all times, as a matter of basic principle.

In the current period when it has become popular to

slander communism, it's important to point out the great feats that were accomplished under its red banner.

As the famed scientist Albert Einstein – himself a socialist – once put it, "Without Russia, those blood dogs would have obtained their goal, or in any case, would have been close to it."

The Nazi's rise to power

Hitler's rise to power in Germany was the result of the combination of a number of social, political, and economic circumstances which we can't explain in much detail in this article.

It is important to note however, that Hitler's Nazi Party -- which was funded in part by prominent American capitalists like Henry Ford and William Hearst -- came to power as a part of a coalition of right-wing conservative parties.

It is also important to remember that the one group of people that opposed the rise of fascism from the very beginning were communists. Among the millions of people that the Nazis persecuted, tortured, and murdered, communists were the very first. It was also communists who formed resistance armies throughout Europe to fight the Nazi's expansion. These liberation armies inflicted heavy damages on the fascists in countries like Greece and Albania, and in the case of Yugoslavia, completely defeated them.

Those who fight for communism – the ideology of the working class and oppressed – fight for the revolutionary overthrow of capitalism and the creation of a free, just, and equal society which operates in the interest of meeting human need, and fight against fascism, an extreme version of capitalism in which society is run by a right wing dictatorship made up of a merging of the government and business leadership, that utilizes fear mongering, ultranationalism, and force to maintain its rule.

Italian dictator Benito Mussolini, the first fascist in power, himself defined fascism as an ideology in opposition to communism: "Granted that the 19th century was the century of socialism, liberalism, democracy, this does not mean that the 20th century must also be the century of socialism, liberalism, democracy. Political doctrines pass; nations remain. We are free to believe that this is the century of authority, a century tending to the 'right', a Fascist century."

The Fascists attack the USSR

After first invading Poland, Denmark, Norway, France, Belgium, the Netherlands, Luxembourg, Greece, and Yugoslavia, Germany invaded the USSR in the largest surprise attack in history on June 22, 1941. The Soviets were largely unprepared for the attack and suffered a number of early losses.

In a stunning example of the superiority of a planned economy, the Soviets were able to dismantle entire factories in the east and ship them the Ural mountains where they were reassembled and reopened.

The fascist German army attacked the Soviet Union in three directions, moving towards Leningrad, Moscow, and the Caucasus simultaneously.

As the entire population of the USSR was mobilized for wartime production, the Soviets were able to produce much needed resources and weapons. While the invading German army had pushed to occupy Moscow before winter, they were defeated by a series of counter-attacks by the Red Army at the outskirts of the city.

Weakened by the defeat, the Germans regrouped and then rerouted their drive into the southern USSR. The Germans wanted to control the fertile and oil-rich Caucasus and damage the Soviet economy by severing its transportation from Central Asia along the Volga River.

As they moved south, the German forces were split in two on Nazi leader Adolf Hitler's orders. The first group continued advancing south towards the Caucasus while the second group moved east towards the Volga River and the city of Stalingrad.

Hitler wanted to capture Stalingrad for a few reasons. First, Stalingrad was a major industrial city which sat on the banks of the Volga River, a vital transportation route as mentioned above. The capture of the city would also secure the left side of the section of the army advancing into the Caucasus. Finally, Hitler though the capture of a city named after the leader of a country with an ideology (communism) completely opposed to his own (Nazism) would serve as positive propaganda for Germany.

The Germans continued to push the Red Army back, until finally establishing defensive lines made up of the Armies of their Italian, Hungarian, and Romanian allies. The German 6th Army was only kilometers away from Stalingrad and was planning to make its attack.

Attack on Stalingrad

Once the Nazi's plan became clear, the Soviets began plans to defend Stalingrad at all costs and turn the German war machine back once and for all.

Red Army units moving eastward were sent to the city where they joined up with additional Soviet troops who had arrived on the Volga River to form the 62nd Army. Men, women, and children who lived in the city, and were determined to defend their country and socialist system, bravely volunteered to build trenches and fortified barriers.

On August 23, 1942, the Germans launched a massive air bombardment of Stalingrad which caused a firestorm that killed thousands of civilians and turned the city into ruins. Eighty percent of the city's living space was completely destroyed.

The 1077th Anti-aircraft regiment, which was made up of young women volunteers, bravely defended Stalingrad from the German attackers. Even though they had little training battling ground units and no support from other Soviet units, the heroic women stood strong and took on the advancing German Panzer tanks head on. The 16th Panzer Division was held off for some time before it was finally able to destroy the Anti Aircraft batteries.

By the end of August the German army had set up to the north and south of Stalingrad. At this point the city was still relying on its workers militias – which were made up of Soviets not directly involved in wartime production – as its main line of defense.

The workers of Stalingrad showed an amazing amount of courage that is a true testament to the power of the working class. Even as bombs dropped and bullets flew around them, the workers continued to produce tanks, which were manned by crews of volunteers who immediately drove them directly from the factory floor to the front lines.

In early September the Soviet 62nd Army formed defense lines amongst the rubble of the devastated city, causing the advancing Germans to suffer heavy losses.

Under intense and unending bombardment, Soviet reinforcements began to arrive across the Volga River from the eastern bank. Fighting was becoming increasingly bitter and fierce, to such a degree that the life expectancy of newly arrived Soviet soldiers dropped to less than 24 hours.

The Soviet military's leaders soon adopted a new method of combat. By moving in as close as possible to the enemy units on the ground they were able to limit the Nazi's air attack, which was held back by the Germans out of the fear that they may have hit their own soldiers. Because of this new method, the Germans were forced into bloody fights for every street, factory, building, and house.

At the Grain Elevator on Mamayev Kurgan, a hill above the city where much of the bloody fighting occurred, the Nazi and Soviet soldiers were so close they could hear each other breathe. The fight for that Grain Elevator went on for weeks until the Germans finally destroyed it.

In another part of Stalingrad, an apartment building which would later be known as "Pavlov's House" was turned into an impenetrable fortress by a Red Army platoon under the command of Yakov Pavlov.

German tanks were rendered useless because they couldn't move through the large piles of rubble which filled the city. The Soviets on the other hand used the ruins to their advantage. Soviet soldiers used heaps of concrete as defensive barriers while Soviet snipers, many of whom were women, hid in them. The snipers were particularly successful, inflicting heavy casualties on the Nazis.

Despite this, the Germans were finally able to capture 90% of the city by November. The Soviets however refused to surrender, and fierce fighting continued. While the Soviet troops fought to defend buildings like the Red October steel factory, Soviet workers went on repairing tanks and weapons in what had become the middle of the battlefield.

It was at this time that the Soviets began planning their counter attack. Large numbers of Soviet forces were concentrated to the north and south of Stalingrad. The Soviets planned to pin down the German troops in Stalingrad while penetrating the weak German defenses around the city, and then surrounding it.

On November 19, the Red Army launched a full scale attack. Massive numbers of soldiers and tanks broke through the German's defensive lines to the north, which were held by the 3rd Romanian Army.

The next day a second offensive was launched to the

south of the city, this time against a defensive line being held by the Romanian 4th Army Corps. The Romanian forces were defeated almost immediately, and the Soviet soldiers moved to encircle the city.

The Red Army units trapped about 250,000 German, Croatian, and Romanian soldiers inside the city, which they then stormed.

Having announced in a speech only a month earlier that the Germans would never leave Stalingrad, Hitler ordered his fascist soldiers not to surrender under any circumstances, despite the fact that they were trapped inside the city.

After defeating an attack from a group of Germans from the south, the Soviets tightened their circle around the city and continued to advance.

Communist victory

The Soviets gave the fascist troops a chance to surrender – which they refused – and then launched another attack.

Hitler promoted the commander of the 6th army, Friedrich Paulus, to field marshal on January 30, 1943. Since no German field marshal had ever surrendered or been captured, Hitler hoped that Paulus would fight to the death. He was wrong.

As the Red Army closed in on Paulus' headquarters in what was left of a department store, the fascists surrendered. A total of 91,000 fascist soldiers – including 22 generals – were taken captive by the Soviets.

This monumental defeat at the hands of the Red Army was the beginning of the end for the Nazis.

The defeat of Nazi Germany

After their victory at Stalingrad, the Red Army launched a serious of offensives through the winter aimed at liberating the territory occupied by the Germans.

In July the Germans launched a final offensive against the USSR at Kursk, but the Soviets knew about the attack in advance and launched a counteroffensive that pushed the fascist army back.

In June of 1944, days after allied troops landed at Normandy on "D-Day", the Red Army launched Operation Bagration, an offensive involving 2.5 million men and 6,000 tanks. Finland couldn't be defended against the Soviet advance and was forced to sign a ceasefire.

Although the Western allies were beginning to win battles against the Nazis in Western Europe, many historians have pointed out that the Red Army's advance was so powerful by that time that it could have defeated Germany alone.

The Red Army and 78,556 soldiers of the 1st Polish Army began their final assault on Berlin, the capital of Germany, on April 16, 1945. The Soviets had defeated the Nazis in a series of battles in their advance, the German Army was now in full retreat, and most of the Nazi leaders had either been killed or captured.

In a final act of desperation before committing suicide, Hitler called for all Germans, including children, to join militias and fight against the Red Army.

Berlin fell to the Red Army on May 2, 1945, and the Hammer and Sickle was flown over the Reichstag. Within days all German forces unconditionally surrendered.

Hail the Red Army!

On this 63rd anniversary of the Nazi's defeat at

90

Stalingrad, the Revolutionary Youth wish to offer our sincerest gratitude to the heroic Soviet people who gave everything they had to defeat the Nazi monster and encourage all youths, workers, and other oppressed people around the world to do the same.

The Nicaraguan Revolution: From Liberation to Betrayal

In 1979, forces of the Frente Sandinista Liberacion Nacional, or Sandinista National Liberation Front (FSLN), rolled triumphantly into Managua, Nicaragua, after overthrowing the hated dictatorship of Anastasio Somoza Debayle.

The FSLN had struggled for nearly two decades to oust the U.S.-backed Somoza dynasty, which brutally repressed and exploited the Nicaraguan people before finally being successful.

Background

Nicaragua had long been dominated by foreign powers, from Spain to the United States.

In the 1920's, a miner named Augusto César Sandino formed an army of workers and peasants to fight alongside liberal forces in the army against a presidential regime installed by the U.S. Eventually the U.S. forced a cease-fire between the liberal leaders and the regime they had installed, but Sandino refused to stop fighting. Instead, he reorganized his army to fight the "Colossus to the North." His forces battled against U.S. Marines sent to capture him for some time, with various degrees of success. As he continued to carry out his anti-imperialist struggle, Sandino received the support of the Communist International and workers and farmers all over the world. After spending a brief period in Mexico, where he tried to reorganize and get material aid from a number of Latin American leaders and forces, Sandino returned to Nicaragua.

The U.S. withdrew its forces in 1933, as the Great Depression greatly weakened its ability to intervene in Latin America. But the U.S. left behind a terrible legacy: the National

Guard, led by a man named Anastasio Somoza.

Sandino agreed to disarm his forces as a new president was elected in Nicaragua; but after doing so he was betrayed by Somoza's National Guard, which ambushed him as he was on his way to Managua to negotiate an end to the fighting.

The next day, the National Guard massacred cooperative farmers that belonged to Sandinista's army.

Somoza went on to name himself leader of the country two years later, after forcing Nicaragua's president to resign.

He ruled with an iron fist and set up a repressive system that would later be taken over by his son Luis in 1956, then another son, Anastasio Somoza Debayle, in 1967.

The 1972 earthquake and 'Hurricane Somoza'

On December 23, 1972, a devastating earthquake struck Managua, the capital city of Nicaragua, killing 10,000 and leaving another 250,000 homeless.

International aid came in from around the world, but it was almost all kept by Anastasio Somoza Debayle and his National Guard. Somoza, who by that time controlled hundreds of millions of dollars (all 'made' through his exploitation of the country and its workers and farmers), didn't even rebuild parts of the capital that had been destroyed!

The audacity of Somoza caused many, such as business owners, who didn't oppose his rule previous to join the millions of workers and farmers who did. At this point, his rule was all but over.

A different kind of house party

In December, 1974, a group of FSLN members stormed a house where the Minister of Agriculture was having a party.

They took the party's attendees, many of whom were related to Somoza, hostage and demanded a $1 million ransom, the release of 14 political prisoners (including Daniel Ortega, who would later become president), the printing of their official communiqué in the newspaper *La Prensa* (and the reading of its contents over the radio), and a raise in the wages of the National Guard. The government was forced to meet all of their demands but the last.

Afterwards, Somoza stepped up the political repression and physical attacks on all who opposed him. Torture and censorship were the norm under Tachito, as he was commonly known, and yet the U.S. government continued to support him.

During this period, many FSLN members were killed, including its leader, Carlos Fonseca Amador.

A split in the ranks

Over the next period, the FSLN would split into three pieces. The different groups, divided over the best approach to overthrow Somoza, continued to carry on their struggle.

In 1977, a group known as "The Twelve," made up of business leaders, clergy and professionals opposed to Somoza formed, allied with the Terceristas, or "third way" split (as opposed to the other groups that thought either a prolonged struggle based in rural areas, or a struggle based mainly on workers in the cities was the best way forward).

In 1978, Pedro Joaquín Chamorro Cardenal, the editor of La Prensa and leader of a capitalist opposition party called the Democratic Union of Liberation, was assassinated. Evidence pointed at Somoza, his son, and other members of the National Guard. Riots broke out all over the country and business owners – eager to have Somoza replaced with someone who would better and more efficiently represent their interests – organized a mass shut down of the economy.

The Terceristas then carried out a number of operations. At one point, they took the entire Nicaraguan Congress hostage and were able to have their call for a national uprising broadcast.

In a few days, uprisings took place in six cities across the country. Members of all three splinters of the FSLN joined armed and semi-armed workers and farmers as they struggled to oust Somoza.

In early 1979, U.S. President Jimmy Carter withdrew support for Somoza, sensing a victory for the FSLN was imminent.

Instead, he put his support behind the so-called Broad Opposition Front (FAO, according to its initials in Spanish), a capitalist, pro-U.S. grouping made up of members of the Democratic Union of Liberation and "The Twelve." Together, they worked out a plan to replace Somoza with a transitional government that would not include the FSLN.

In early 1979, U.S. President Jimmy Carter, sensing that a victory for the FSLN was imminent, withdrew support for Somoza. Instead, he put his support behind the so-called Broad Opposition Front (FAO, according to its initials in Spanish), a capitalist, pro-U.S. Grouping made up of members of the Democratic Union of Liberation and "The Twelve."

Together, they worked out a plan to replace Somoza with a transitional government that would not include the FSLN.

"The Twelve," likely accepting the fact that the Sandinistas were growing in power and size and could carry on a successful struggle against the FAO (the workers and farmers were clear they didn't want "Somocism without Somoza"), ended up withdrawing from it. Instead, they formed a "National Patriotic Front" with the "United People's Movement."

The three splinters of the FSLN continued to grow, gaining thousands of members and stepping up their activities, until they finally reunited on March 7, 1979. The newly reformed FSLN was led by a National Directorate with three members from each of the three splinters.

The final insurrection

The FSLN, which was once one of many groups opposed to Somoza's dictatorship, has by now become the leading force.

Still early in 1979, they opened five separate guerrilla fronts which battled the National Guard on a daily basis.

On June 4, an indefinite general strike was called and the FSLN launched an insurrection in Managua. Twelve days later, the creation of a "government in exile" – made up of Daniel Ortega from the FSLN, Moisés Hassan Morales from the FPN, Sergio Ramírez Mercado of "The Twelve", Alfonso Robelo Callejas of the "National Democratic Movement" and Violeta Barrios de Chamorro, the widow of assassinated *La Prensa* editor Pedro Joaquín Chamorro Cardenal – inneighboring Costa Rica was announced.

By the end of June, most of the territory outside of Managua was under FSLN control, and the government in exile released a program promising democratic reform and freedom for all but those who advocated the return of Somoza. Somoza himself resigned and boarded a plane for Miami on July 17, 1979.

On July 19, a triumphant FSLN entered Managua, followed two days later by the government in exile.

Revolutionary policy

Under the new government, the immense problems of Nicaragua were finally addressed. With the assistance of revolutionary Cuba (who had helped the FSLN throughout their

96

struggle), Nicaragua began to battle illiteracy (lowering the rate from 50% to 12%), disease (Cuba doctors are nurses tended to countless Nicaraguans – many who had never seen a doctor in their lives – and helped eliminate polio), lack of education (Cuban teachers and Nicaraguan volunteers provided basic education and job training), underdevelopment (Cuba provided materials – including an entire sugar mill – to help industrialize the country) and dependency on the U.S. Between 1979 and 1987, Cuba providedNicaragua with over $300 million worth of aid, not counting the education it provided to many Nicaraguans in its schools.

Institutionalized sexism was abolished, thousands of jobs were created, houses were constructed for those that needed them, and subsidies were provided for food.

Overall, the Nicaraguan workers and farmers made immense gains through their hard work and the solidarity of socialist Cuba.

Counterrevolution and defeat

In 1984 Nicaragua had national elections – which were considered "free and fair" by all international observers – in 1984. The FSLN won handily, with Daniel Ortega elected as president and other members winning a majority of seats in the National Assembly.

The U.S. government, however, joined with a number of Nicaraguan capitalists who basically boycotted the election in order to later paint the FSLN as "communist dictators." They organized counterrevolutionary bands, or contras, into one body. This group, which was heavily funded by the U.S. government, inflicted terror on the Nicaraguan people for years.

Through this period it was necessary to push the revolution forward, with the power of the workers and farmers, to take the means of production (the tools and technology used to produce the goods people want

and need) and the land out of the hands of the capitalist parasites and complete the socialist revolution. Instead, the leadership of the FSLN gradually transformed the revolutionary front into a liberal political party.

In 1990, things were stagnating. Many thought that if the FSLN stayed in power the contras would keep killing and conditions would worsen. Violeta Chamorro ran against Ortega in the presidential elections and received 55% of the votes. It was all over.

The second time as a farce

Daniel Ortega was elected president of Nicaragua again in 2006. Now, he claims to have "lost Marx and found God." In practice, this means that he has become a traitor to the workers and farmers of Nicaragua. Proof of this lies in a recent law banning all abortion, even when a women has been raped or is in medical danger.

Ortega still has to pose as a leftist to some extent, as the millions who support the FSLN expect it; but in reality, he is little more than an opportunist sell-out. There are still many in the rank-and-file of the FSLN who are capable of and renewing the struggle for socialism.

They must break free from Ortega and his cronies, and organize the toiling masses of Nicaragua once again. In the spirit of Sandino!

Always low wages, always Wal-Mart

Its annual sales of more than $250 billion make Wal-Mart larger, economically speaking, than Indonesia, the world's fourth most populous nation. Including the value of stock received, Wal-Mart CEO H. Lee Scott's pay package soared to an amazing $12.44 million in 2004. So why then are his 1.3 his million Wal-Mart employees, seventy percent of whom are women, paid so poorly that they can't afford the basic necessities of life?

Wal-Mart, the largest private employer in the United States, pays it's employees an average of $9.64 an hour if they are full-time employees, according to *Business Week*. Yet even those full-time workers, who comprise only about 66% of Wal-Mart's workforce, may be scheduled for as few 34 hours weekly. Even at $9.64 hourly (which many cite as a very generous estimate), working 34 hours a week, a Wal-Mart employee earns only $17,043 annually, well under the $18,850 federal poverty guideline for a family of four in 2004. Using published studies on an "adequate but austere" budget for a family with one adult, one preschooler, and one school-aged child living in Salina, Kansas, writer Stan Cox conducted his own study into the possibility of a single mother supporting herself and her two children while working as a cashier at the local Wal-Mart ('A Wal-Mart wage doesn't go very far -- even at Wal-Mart' *Alternet* June 10, 2003). "We calculated the amount that our hypothetical three-member family would spend each month if as many of its essential needs as possible were supplied by our local Supercenter. Despite our best efforts, we exceeded our cashier's monthly income by $146". This, even after they "slashed some of the published budget items as much as 38%, based on the 'Always Low Prices' we found at the Supercenter", and despite the fact that "we couldn't have come that close had our cashier's family not been eligible for a State of Kansas child-care allowance that covers all but $22 per month in child-care costs for a such a family living on so low a wage", and that "Our cost-cutting left no room for 'luxuries': no travel outside of Saline County, no cable TV, no home telephone service, no movies, no newspaper or magazine subscriptions, no fees for community sports or classes, no saving at Wal-Mart's in-store bank in case the car had to be replaced, no eating out ... Most of what's available at the Supercenter was off-limits to us".

In her book "Nickel and Dimed", a first-hand account of trying to make a living in four working class jobs in four cities, one of them a Minneapolis Wal-Mart, Babara Ehrenreich recalls that one of her co-workers at the store constantly checked the price of a T-shirt (the type Wal-Mart required its employees to wear) to see if it was on sale, because she couldn't afford to buy the Wal-Mart shirt on a Wal-Mart salary.

So, how do jobs at Wal-Mart compare to those of other employers? An October 2003 AFL-CIO report finds that "While 66 percent of workers at large U.S. firms get health coverage on the job, fewer than half of Wal-Mart workers do"; and if union grocery workers' wages were slashed to match the wages of Wal-Mart workers, their communities would lose between $1.6 billion and $3 billion annually. Wal-Mart's virulent, and sometimes even unlawful, anti-union policies (also in her book *Nickel and Dimed*, Barbara Ehrenreich reports that when new employees start at Wal-Mart, they must first watch a video warning them against joining a union) prevent workers from earning family-supportive wages and benefits. According to a 2002 report by the Institute for Women's Policy Research, unionized workers in the retail food industry made more than 30 percent in hourly wages more than their nonunion counterparts.

While Wal-Mart keeps its workers in a state of poverty, they also impoverish entire communities. An analysis by the United Food and Commercial Workers shows that "In the top 100 cities where Wal-Mart's share of the grocery industry grew more than 20 percent between 1998 and 2002, the number of

100

cashier jobs fell as much as 2.3 percent. And every time Wal-Mart expanded its market share by 1 percent in the grocery business, retail food cashiers' wages dropped an average of 5.5 cents per hour." An October 2003 report prepared for the city of Los Angeles concludes that as Supercenters tend to convert communities' union-scale retail jobs to fewer lower-paying retail jobs, the difference in overall compensation is "as much as $8 an hour."

Women receive even lower wages than their male counterparts at Wal-Mart. While working in a Pinellas Park, Florida Wal-Mart, Ramonda Scott was told that the reason men doing similar work earned more than she did was that men came there to make careers, and housewives just needed to earn spending money. A class action lawsuit was filed on behalf of more than 1 million women, including those currently working at Wal-Mart's more than 3,000 stores. Documents of the lawsuit describe a corporation in which women are paid lower wages and promoted less than their male equals, and where women are steered into "female" departments, including requiring them to retrieve coffee for their male counterparts. There are also reports that those who dare complain about their unequal treatment are demoted.

Keeping all of this in mind, the wages Wal-Mart payes its employees in the United States seem outstanding in comparison to those paid by many of its suppliers around the world. While "Daring to Save You Even More" Wal-Mart supports, and even encourages this by forcing its suppliers to lower costs by any means, threatening to take their business elsewhere. A Bangladeshi factory worker who makes clothing for Wal-Mart would be hard pressed to make even a single purchase at a Supercenter.

While Wal-Mart often implies that any raise in wages paid to their workers would hinder their ability to continue to provide such low prices to consumers, according to the UFCW, if Wal-Mart paid each employee $1 an hour more, it could maintain its profitability level by increasing prices a mere half penny per dollar. This would mean the price of a $2 pair of socks would increase to $2.01.

This is the face of capitalist America, embodied by its largest private employer, exploiting the working class in it's never ending quest for profit.

Murder, it's the real thing: Coca-Cola can't hide its crimes in Colombia

Fifteen year-old David Jose Carranza Calle -- son of Limberto Carranza, a Colombian Coca-Cola worker who is the national director of Sinaltrainal (the union of Colombian Coca-Cola workers) -- was riding his bicycle at around noon in a place known as Simon Bolivar Blvd., (La Tienda la Esmeralda) in Barranquilla, Colombia, when suddenly four masked subjects pulled him from his bicycle and forced him into a white truck. They proceeded to take him to an unknown location where they tortured him, asking the whereabouts of his father. The torture lasted until about 4:30 p.m., when they dropped him on the side of the road where he was found by a man passing by. Meanwhile, Limberto Carranze received a phone call at his home in which he was told: "Unionist son of a bitch; we are going to break you. And if you won't break, we will attack your home."

While this sounds like it could be right out of a movie, unfortunately it's all too real. This is what happened on September 10th, 2003, and is just one of many attacks on Coca-Cola workers in "a country where belonging to a union is like carrying a tombstone on your back".

Since 1989, eight union leaders from four separate bottling plants in Colombia have been murdered, and hundreds of other workers and their families have been tortured, kidnapped and/or illegally detained by violent paramilitaries, often working closely with plant managements.

Isidro Segundo Gil was one of the unfortunate victims of such violence. An employee at a Coca-Cola bottling plant in Carepa, Colombia, he was killed at his workplace by paramilitary thugs. Eyewitness accounts provided a chilling description of his assassination in which thugs showed up at the Carepa plant gate and fired 10 shots at Gil, a member of the union executive board, mortally wounding him. An hour later, another leader was kidnapped at his home. That evening, a building that housed the union's offices, equipment and records was set ablaze. Isidro's children are now forced to live in hiding with relatives in fear that they themselves may be next.

The day after the murder of Isidro, a heavily armed group returned to the plant, called the workers together and told them if they didn't quit the union by 4p.m., they too would be killed. Resignation forms were prepared in advance by Coca-Cola's plant manager, who had a history of socializing with the paramilitaries and had earlier "given (them) an order to carry out the task of destroying the union", according to a lawsuit filed against Coca-Cola, Pan-American Beverages (the largest soft drink bottler in Latin America) and Bebidas y Alimentos (A bottler owned by Richard Kirby of Key Biscayne, Fla., which operates the plant in which Gil was killd), by Sinaltrainal, the International Labor Rights Fund (ILRF) and the United Steelworkers of America. The lawsuit asserts that Coke bottlers "contracted with or otherwise directed paramilitary security forces that utilized extreme violence and murdered, tortured, unlawfully detained or otherwise silenced trade union leader." The attacks at the Carepa plant lead to union members resigning *en masse* and fleeing the area, fearing for their lives. The company broke off contract negotiations while the paramilitaries camped outside the plant gate for the next two months, and the union was crushed. Experienced workers who made about $380 a month were replaced by new hires earning minimum wage ($130 a month).

No charges were ever filed against Gil's killers or those who killed at least seven other Coca-Cola unionists; and Coca-Cola, while tightly controlling the manufacture and distribution of its products overseas and collecting the profits, denies any responsibility to workers.

"It shocks the conscience that these companies seek to immunize themselves from charges of human rights violation," says ILRF attorney Terry Collingsworth.

While workers at Coke bottling plants in Colombia continue to risk their lives every day simply by going to work, a few corporate power brokers at Coca-Cola and Atlanta-based SunTrust Banks continue to profit, even while they stand accused as accessories to a violent crime wave.

The world's largest beverage company recently launched a $250 million U.S. advertising blitz on behalf its flagship brand, keyed to the theme, "Coca-Cola...Real." while continually refusing to acknowledge the horrific reality that Colombian Coke workers and their families are facing.

Javier Correa, president of Sinaltrainal says, "We want justice. We want people to know the truth about what is going on in Colombia against Coke workers. Now that you know, will please help us?"

On Nationalism, Socialism, and Communism

A letter on on nationalism, socialism, and communism

To Ricardo Santiago,

Recently I was given some materials from the Free People's Movement, including some of your writings, and it seems to me that you and your organization encourage people to forget about their nationalities altogether - to trade in their identities for that of 'workers'.

Not all nationalism is bad. Aggressive nationalism yes, but we can't let the examples of others lead us to deny our cultures. So yeah, just because you choose not to shout it from the rooftops doesn't stop it from being your identity. If your organization has the whole Che/Castro mentality, I think nationalism preserves the proletariat (working class).

I'm not a socialist or a communist. I enjoy my place among the classes of society (perhaps because I am programmed to chase the luxuries of the capitalist world and I remain forever fantasizing of the possibility of living out the "American Dream", which by the way is forever changing). For that, I suppose you can label me selfish (i.e. to want enjoy the fruits of my labor while an astounding percentage of individuals in New York City remain illiterate), and so be it. My opinion, is that socialism/communism within the scope of reality fails to "do it" for me.

Yes, free health care, education, etc. is great; but I don't want to work my ass of and have exactly what everyone else has. How can you expect an unrewarding work ethic to motivate the working class (everyone)?

Signed,

A Working Puerto Rican Woman - New York, NY

Ricardo's reply

First, let me say that I'm glad you took the time and energy to write me to express your thoughts. Constant dialogue with, and participation of, the people is vital to our organization as we are based in the broad masses.

You stated in your letter that "not all nationalism is bad." For the most part I would disagree. For our cause, nationalism is bad, and always will be. It's roots are based in the fairly recent (historically speaking) rise of the modern nation-state. Nationalism -- a sense of national pride which is usually accompanied with a sense of 'superiority' over other nationalities -- serves to separate, and increase separation of, the workers of the world. So, as an internationalist (yes, just like Che), I must be directly opposed to nationalism. We make the call for the "Workers of the world [to] unite", not just the "Workers of Panama."

Of course, it should go without saying that we stand in support of national independence movements which stand in opposition to imperialism and neocolonialism.

I must admit that I'm not completely sure what you mean by "preserving" the proletariat. The goal is to abolish ALL classes -- that is, to create a classless, and thus equal, society. This is accomplished through revolution in which the working class takes power by taking control of the means of production and establishing socialism, under which class antagonisms can be eliminated thus paving the way for egalitarian society.

You touched on what you call a 'Che/Castro' mentality, and seemed to ask if our organization 'had' it. The answer would be to a large extent yes. We agree on many more things than we disagree on, and we understand that in the conditions that it faced and continues to face, Cuba has accomplished more than most anyone would have thought possible.

Ernesto 'Che' Guevara directly participated in revolutionary war in several nations, none of which were his own. To quote him, "And let us develop a true proletarian internationalism; with international proletarian armies; the flag under which we fight would be the sacred cause of redeeming humanity. To die under the flag of Vietnam, of Venezuela, of Guatemala, of Laos, of Guinea, of Colombia, of Bolivia, of Brazil -- to name only a few scenes of today's armed struggle -- would be equally glorious and desirable for an American, an Asian, an African, even a European."

It could be argued that Fidel uses nationalism and nationalist rhetoric in order to mobilize and unite the Cuban people in the process of defending the revolution against the US imperialist aggressors. It should also be noted that a large part of the nationalist sentiments that exist in Cuba are born directly of the United State's long history of meddling in Cuba's internal affairs. As Marxists, Fidel, as well as the Communist Party of Cuba and the Cuban people, have a great internationalist spirit. This is evident by the various work Cuba has done internationally -- supporting and supplying revolutionaries and independence fighters (in Grenada, Several in Africa and Central America), and sending volunteer doctors to work in underdeveloped countries around the world (Haiti, Venezuela, and throughout Africa).

So back to the original topic, the ideology of our movement is Marxism, a major aspect of which is internationalism, and which is a living and constantly developing scientific revolutionary theory.

Do I think you are selfish? Obviously I don't know you

well enough to make such a judgment. A better question would probably be do I blame those who are "American dreaming"? The answer is of course not, as it born of systematic indoctrination more than any sort of "evil." The entire capitalist system is designed to create a certain (bourgeois) mentality. The actual fact is that you do not enjoy the fruits of your labor, as no member of the working class does. Our exploitation is what fuels the capitalist system (ie. Profits which are derived DIRECTLY from the exploitation of workers and nowhere else). For more on this see "Wage Labour and Capital" by Karl Marx, or my own introductory essays "The Ills of Capitalism" and "The Haves and the Have-nots".

You also stated in your letter "My opinion, is that socialism/communism within the scope of reality fails to "do it" for me." I'm not sure if I fully understand what you're trying to express here either, but the 'reality' is that Marxism is based upon a correct analysis of historical development -- historical materialism [See Frederick Engels "Socialism Utopian and Scientific"]. Although healthcare & education would be available under socialism or communism, the benefits would be so much more. In fact, healthcare & education are free in many Capitalist countries today (though not the US). Communism is achieved when we have abolished all class antagonisms and when we have created a society in which people are not alienated from the products of their labor.

Communism will be the end result when the working class (the majority) gain class consciousness, and understand that the capitalist system operates in the interest of, and is controlled by, the capitalist class (the elite minority). When the correct consciousness is reached, revolution is inevitable, just as the bourgeois gained the consciousness to realize that the feudal social system stood in opposition to their class interests, thus leading to the bourgeois revolutions in France, USA, etc. that lead to the establishment of capitalism. The main difference is of course that the interest of the working class is to take control of the means of production and to suppress the capitalist class --

eliminating class antagonisms and eventually class divisions all together.

You wrote "I don't want to work my ass off and have exactly what everyone else has." Currently, the three richest people in the world control more wealth than everyone in the poorest 28 nations COMBINED. Under capitalism wealth is concentrated in the hands of very few. What this means, is that in an egalitarian society, the vast majority of people will have much MORE than they currently have -- even though they're "working their asses off" now. When socialism is realized, profit motives disappear, and work is undertaken to meet the needs of society -- this includes the participation of EVERYONE (those working now, the rich who do nothing productive, and the vast number of unemployed) in the production process -- this leads to a much shorter and less intense working day.

Finally, you asked "How can you expect an unrewarding work ethic to motivate the working class (everyone)?" While not everyone belongs to the working class, it's true that most do. When socialism has been established all class divisions will begin to dissolve and the working class along with it. "Greed" and the "quest for more" will no longer be the main motivation for working. Under capitalism the biggest motivation for working is simply fulfilling one's basic needs (food, shelter, etc) -- and indeed, many struggle even for that. When the fulfillment of these basic needs are guaranteed humans can finally fully and freely develop. People will not want to loose the guarantee of their basic needs, and the only insurance of the prosperity of all will be the contribution of all ("From each according to their ability, to each according to their need"). People are not inherently greedy -- greed has been systematically instilled into them.

Hopefully I was able to reply in a manner you find satisfactory. I encourage you to read more materials from our organization, and to contact us again anytime you wish.

110

Communist Perspectives on North Korea

The question of Korea comes up often in the political life of revolutionaries.

The northern part of the peninsula is pointed to by right-wingers and many left-wingers as a totalitarian hellhole that stands in stark contrast to the "democratic" and prosperous south. Still a handful of others claiming to be "anti-revisionist communists" hold up north Korea as a shining example of socialism. Little analysis or facts are put forward by any of sides to defend their arguments.

It is of vital importance for us to understand the situation in Korea and its relation to the rest of the world.

Korea was annexed by imperialist Japan in 1910 and remained under its control (via a brutal occupation) until Japan's defeat in World War II.

An agreement was reached between the USSR and the U.S., who were at the time in a military alliance against Germany and Japan, that each country would occupy one-half of the Korean Peninsula while preparations for independence were made.

Koreans set up a provisional government on their own, but the U.S. refused to recognize it fearing communist influence (a heroic resistance was fought against the Japanese largely under the leadership and influence of Korean communists, and communist ideas subsequently spread throughout the masses of workers and farmers in Korea).

A section of the U.S. military ran Korea instead, leaving the collaborationist Koreans who helped administer the country under the Japanese occupation in their positions. Although Japan had surrendered in 1945, Japanese officials remained in

Korea under the watch of the U.S. military rulers until 1946.

A new government was eventually established in a sham election in 1948 which was boycotted by all left-wing parties and held only in the southern, U.S.-occupied half of the country. Syngman Rhee, a virulent anti-communist who had recently returned from the U.S. (where he lived for years) emerged as president of the southern half of Korea, with the full approval and backing of the U.S. government.

Propped-up by the U.S. military forces in the region, Rhee's government carried out a bloody campaign of terror against workers and farmers under the banner of "eliminating communism." Some 100,000 Korean lost their lives while countless others were tortured.

In the northern part of the peninsula, a temporary "Civil Authority" under the USSR's military was set up in 1945, while "provisional committees" were established across the region by Koreans. With the backing of the present military forces of the USSR a social revolution took place. Property owned by Japanese capitalists and their collaborators was seized and redistributed to poor farmers, local landlords saw their land holdings reduced to plots equal in size to that of the poor farmers, and key industries were taken into public ownership. In short order, imperialist domination had been thrown off, capitalist rule had been smashed, and the expropriators were expropriated. In 1946, a Provisional People's Committee was proclaimed, with Kim Il-Sung – a leader of the guerrilla war against the Japanese occupation – as its leader. The forces of the USSR withdrew in 1948.

While the revolutionary transformation that occurred in the north was no doubt genuine, its reliance on the soldiers of the USSR, which was by then a bureaucratized proletarian state (that is, a state in which a privileged bureaucratic caste, having excluded the working class from power, rules over collectivized property born out of the overthrow of capitalist rule and property relations) and the leadership of Kim Il-Sung and his cohorts who looked to the USSR as it then existed as the model of "socialism," resulted in the creation of bureaucratic proletarian state as opposed to a normal proletarian state, in which the working class would have ruled directly. Soon after Syngman Rhee unilaterally proclaimed the Republic of Korea (ROK) in the south on August 15, 1948, Kim Il-Sung proclaimed the Democratic People's Republic of Korea (DPRK) in the north on September 9.

A series of cross-border skirmishes between the two sides followed. Finally, on June 25, 1950, the DPRK invaded the south in response to one such cross-border attack with the goal of liberating the south from the rule of the collaborators and imperialist-puppets and reunifying the country. Even after the murder of 100,000 suspected leftists by the Rhee regime, the invasion by the DPRK unleashed a social revolution in the south.

Few wanted to defend the puppet Rhee regime. Soldiers in the south Korean army abandoned their posts en masse. Many south Korean soldiers switched sides and began fighting alongside their comrades from the north. Pilots in the south Korean military flew their planes to airfields in the north and south Korean captains sailed their ships to ports there.

Within days the south Korean military had crumbled. On June 28, forces of the DPRK took Seoul, capital of the south.

The U.S. government was quick to intervene, but it was to no avail. By August, what was left of the south Korean military and the forces sent by the U.S. government had been driven into the southeastern most part of the peninsula, where they were holding on to a mere 10 percent of the total land.

Shortly after however, the U.S. was able to push a resolution through the United Nations Security Council – which was then being boycotted by the USSR over the exclusion of revolutionary China in favor of the nationalist-held island of Taiwan – that called for member states to send troops to assist

113

the ROK. Several countries agreed and sent forces which fought under the command of U.S. forces, which greatly increased their size in Korea after the UN resolution. This manipulation of the UN, which had no business intervening in a civil war to begin with, exposed its role as a "fig leaf" cover for imperialism.

The U.S. forces and its allies were able to push the DPRK's military back across the original line of division and nearly into China.

In response to the invasion of Korea by foreign soldiers and threats by the U.S. government against China (including the threat of nuclear annihilation), a volunteer army made up of hundreds of thousands of Chinese people was assembled. The People's Volunteer Army made its way across the border and helped the DPRK forces to push the UN invaders back once again.

The hostilities lasted for just over three years until an armistice was signed in 1953.

By the end, some 36,516 U.S. soldiers were dead. For its part, the U.S. invaders, along with their "democratic" allies, had killed some 3 million Koreans, including around 100,000 innocent civilians. As a result of incessant bombing by UN forces, virtually the entire northern half of the Korean Peninsula laid in ruins.

But the war in Korea is not over. The U.S. refuses to this day to sign a peace treaty and maintains a force of tens of thousands of soldiers and countless heavy weapons in the south. It also has many sanctions against the north and several navy vessels stationed in the waters around it.

Likewise, the oppression of the workers and farmers of the south end didn't end with the official end of hostilities or even the 1960 uprising that forced the dictator Syngman Rhee out of power. Many legacies of Rhee and the U.S.-occupation government, such as the National Security Act – which makes it illegal to "create, possess or distribute materials that promote anti-government ideas" among other things – continue today.

It is only with a proper understanding of all of this that we can draw correct conclusions.

Despite the bureaucratic nature of Kim Il-Sung leadership and the state in the USSR which it modeled itself on, revolutionaries should have fought for the military victory of the DPRK in the Korean war. In any situation in which a proletarian state, bureaucratized or not, comes into conflict with a capitalist state, we must fight for the victory of the former.

A victory for the south would have meant a victory of imperialism on a world scale and a victory of the rule of capital on a local scale. The ability of the DPRK to maintain its existence, even in the face of an all-sided attack, stung the imperialists and opened the way for new revolutionary possibilities.

Today, revolutionaries must defend the DPRK unconditionally *from attack* by the U.S. imperialists and/or the puppet government of the south.

We also defend the gains represented in the bureaucratized proletarian state in the north *without* giving *one bit* of support to the ruling bureaucracy. *In spite* of the immense bureaucratic distortions in the DPRK, which often take on truly bizarre forms, such as the cults of personality around the late Kim Il-Sung and his son and current chief-bureaucrat Kim Jong Il, collectivized property, a monopoly on foreign trade, a planned economy, universal health care and universal education still remain.

These are real gains. Despite bureaucratic inefficiencies, the planned economy enabled the war torn north to surpass the south economically from the end of hostilities in 1953 until the mid-1980's. It was in the early 1990's that the real problems began as a result of severe flooding of the north's already-limited arable land and a loss of trading partners and access to vital resources due to the counterrevolutionary destruction of the USSR and the bureaucratized proletarian states in Eastern Europe. But even then the gains of the revolutionary overthrow of capitalism helped limit what could have been an even bigger crisis, as the UN's Food and Agricultural Organization and World Food Program described in 1996, writing about the "Public Distribution System, which ensured food, albeit at much reduced levels, to the entire population," adding "In Korea, the effects of food shortages have been uniformly spread over the population and the PDS has proven itself to be a highly effective channel for food assistance."

While defending the DPRK and the existing gains there in these respects, we also point out that the bureaucrats that lead it are parasites that mismanage the economy and endanger the very existence of the proletarian state itself.

Key to the defense of the existing gains and the ouster of the bureaucracy in favor of workers control in the DPRK is proletarian revolution in the south and ouster of the U.S. occupying forces. Such a revolution would embolden the workers in the north and eliminate the basis for the bureaucracy, which stands on its military-first "Songun" policy – rationalized by the presence of thousands of U.S. soldiers and weapons on its border – and reactionary, isolationist "Juche" policy of bogus self-reliance.

It is on this basis alone that Korea can be reunified as a genuine workers republic, with a truly democratic system of governance and an economy geared toward meeting human need. The creation of such a republic could spark proletarian revolution in nearby imperialist Japan as well as giving the workers and farmers in China the impetus to oust the bureaucrats feeding off their labor and marking the first waves of a renewed world revolution.

Refusing to defend the DPRK as described, while at the same fighting for the workers there and internationally to take power, would be equivalent to refusing to support a union being attacked by a capitalist government and giving up the struggle for the rank-and-file to take control of it because its president was a traitorous bureaucrat with ties to the bosses.

The Truth About Cuba

Since the victory of the revolution in 1959 Cuba has faced every sort of attack imaginable from the United States government. With the aim of isolating, weakening, and overthrowing the revolution, there have been numerous assassination attempts on Cuba's leaders, threats of nuclear annihilation, spy flights, a mercenary invasion, right-wing terrorist attacks, the introduction of insects and diseases to kill its crops and livestock, and an ongoing propaganda campaign aimed at distorting the truth and turning the American people against Cuba. But one question remains: why?

As Cuban President Fidel Castro explained in a 1976 speech, "The imperialists are pained that Cuba, the attacked and blockaded country they tried to destroy years fifteen ago by a mercenary invasion, is today a solid and indestructible bulwark of the world revolutionary movement, whose example of bravery, dignity, and determination gives encouragement to peoples in their struggle for liberation."
Former U.S. president Jimmy Carter admitted this in 1980, saying, "The real threat of Cuba is that they offer a model to be emulated by people who are dissatisfied with their lot or who are struggling to change things for the better."

So what is the truth about Cuba?

The Making Of A Revolution

Christopher Columbus landed in Cuba in 1492 and claimed the island as a colony of Spain. The Spanish forced the islands native's to convert to Catholicism and to accept the Spanish monarch as their leader, massacring men, women, and children across the island in order to break their will to resist.

They put the natives to work in mines, on plantations, in households as servants, and as soldiers in their army. Forcefully

118

removed from their communities, overworked, underfed, and subjected to new diseases brought from Europe, the natives were nearly exterminated by 1542. Many of Cuba's original inhabitants chose to kill their own children and themselves rather than starve or become slaves of the Spanish.

In the 17th century the Spanish began forcefully capturing Africans and importing them to Cuba as slaves to replace the disappearing natives as workers in mines and on sugar plantations.

The Cuban sugar industry grew immensely when the slaves of the neighboring French colony of Saint-Domingue (now Haiti) launched a victorious rebellion in 1791. Before the revolt, Saint-Domingue had a booming coffee and sugar industry dependent on the labor of African slaves. After 1791, Haiti's sugar production never matched its former level, and Cuba emerged as the world's major sugar producer. This lead Spanish landowners to buy new land, build additional sugar refineries, and carry unprecedented numbers of Africans into Cuba as slaves.

Cubans began fighting for their independence from Spain in the 1860's. And, after a series of wars over many years – as the Cuban independence fighters were finally on the verge of victory – the United States intervened to protect its own "interests".

The U.S. government declared war on Spain in 1898, claiming the Spanish blew up one of its ships (which it didn't), and quickly seized, through battles and the Treaty of Paris, Puerto Rico, the Philippines, and Guam.. The United States occupied Cuba, and the U.S. Army disbanded the patriot army and excluded the Cuban patriots – who had fought 30 years for liberation – from power. For the next fifty years the United States would dominate and exploit Cuba in every way imaginable. The U.S. even refused to end the military occupation of the country unless it accepted the Platt Amendment, which prohibited Cuba from making treaties and alliances with other countries, granted military bases on the island to the United States (including Guantanamo Bay, which it holds to this day against the will of the Cuban people), allowed U.S. intervention on the island whenever instability threatened, and limited Cuba's ability to accept foreign loans.

Although the majority of Cubans opposed the Platt Amendment, a handful of Cuban politicians, who were very friendly toward the U.S., passed it. After a series of fraudulent elections, military coups, and U.S. military interventions, in January 1934, with the encouragement of the U.S. government, Sergeant Fulgencio Batista led a military coup.

Batista, as head of the military, governed from behind the scenes from 1934 to 1940, while a number of puppet politicians served as president. In 1944, Batista retired to the United States.

In 1952, after the terms of two of the most corrupt presidents in Cuban history, Batista returned from the United States to run for president. When it became apparent that he would not win the election, he organized another military coup and became dictator. The Cuban people organized into opposition groups against the dictator everywhere.

A young lawyer and political activist, Fidel Castro, brought together a number of young people who were dedicated to the overthrow of Batista and reinstatement of the Cuban constitution. On July 26, Castro and 150 armed Cuban men and women set out to attack the Moncada Military Barracks in Santiago de Cuba – the country's second largest fortress. Their plan was to suprise attack the barracks, and secure weapons to arm the Cuban people for the overthrow of the dictator. Some of the men and women got lost on the way to the barracks, while many of the ones who did make it were quickly captured by soldiers. Castro and several others escaped, but were later arrested. By Batista's orders, the army brutally tortured and killed 68 insurgents – martyrs who are today heroes in Cuba.

After attempting to defend many of his comrades who

were captured, Castro was put on trial in a hospital under the guard of the military. His defense speech, "History Will Absolve Me" – in which he argued that it was Batista, and not his movement, that violated constitutional law because it took power illegally and tortured and killed prisoners, and in which he promised to lead a revolution that would launch a program of land reform, build houses, offer greater employment opportunities, expand health and welfare services, and nationalize the country's utilities – became the blueprint for his movement. The tribunal sentenced Castro to 15 years in prison.

Fidel and the others in prison built their movement, the "26th of July Movement" (named after the date of their attack on the Moncada Barracks) with the help of supporters throughout Cuba, . After serving two years in prison, Batista was forced by public outcry to release them.

Soon afterward, due to death threats from Batista's forces, Fidel and others from the 26th of July Movement were forced to leave Cuba, and went into exile in Mexico. Knowing there was no way to get rid of the dictator Batista or create a more just society legally, they began to make plans to invade Cuba and begin guerrilla actions.

After raising funds from several sources, including the Cuban community in the U.S., a small farm outside of Mexico City was purchased where the rebels trained. It was around this time that Fidel met the Argentine Ernesto 'Che' Guevara, who agreed to join him within hours.

The Mexican police arrested, and then later released the rebels with the understanding that they would leave the country immediately. This caused the group to hasten their departure.

The 81 guerrillas – including Camilo Cienfuegos, Juan Almeida, and Fidel's brother Raul – crammed themselves into the small yacht Granma, and departed Mexico on the night of November 24, 1956.

Bad weather and other mishaps delayed their arrival by

two days (thus rendering useless an armed uprising in Santiago which was aimed at drawing away the attention of Batista's forces), and caused them to arrive 30 miles away from the point where weapons and reinforcements awaited them.

Almost immediately after their landing, they were ambushed by Batista's troops. All but a dozen of the rebels were killed.

The handful of survivors made their way undetected into the rugged Sierra Maestra mountains. It was from here that their Rebel Army would organize raids on military installations to acquire weapons, working closely with the regions peasants and gaining their full support.

Herbert Matthews, a New York Times correspondent, was invited to the Sierra Maestra to report on the 26th of July Movement. Matthews' reports brought international attention to the movement. New recruits continued to join the rebels, and urban guerrilla groups, such as the Civic Resistance group, founded in 1957, became auxiliaries of the 26th of July Movement.

On March 13, 1957, a group of students, the Revolutionary Directorate, attacked the presidential palace, in an attempt to assassinate Batista. The dictator barely escaped with his life as the rebels shot their way onto the grounds. José Antonio Echeverría, the directorate's leader, was shot and the rest of his men were captured, killed, or forced into hiding. Today they are considered heroes in Cuba.

The Rebel Army continued to win battle after battle as the Cuban people's opposition to Batista increased. In March of 1958, 45 civic organizations signed an open letter supporting the guerrillas.

Columns of troops lead by guerrilla leaders like Che Guevara and Camilo Cienfuegos began to split off from the main army and made their way towards the capital city of Havana, defeating Batista's troops in several battles along the way.

At dawn on January 1st, 1959, after the all-but-complete defeat of the armed forces by the rebels, Batista fled Cuba and left the island in the hands of a military junta.

On January 2nd, the troops of Che Guevara and Camilo Cienfuegos entered Havana, which was paralyzed by a general strike, On January 8th, Fidel entered the city triumphantly and was greeted by thousands upon thousands of joyful Cubans from all over the country.

The United States was hostile towards the revolution from the outset, because it put the interests of the Cuban people above interests of the U.S. Government and American-owned business.

Human Rights

As a part of its propaganda campaign, the United States Government and its agencies have continually accused Cuba of human rights abuses. But when the accomplishments of the Cuban revolution are compared to the actions of the U.S. Government, the truth becomes quite clear.

Fidel Castro himself put it best when he asked, "On what moral grounds can the rulers of a nation in which millionaires and beggars exists; Indians are exterminated; Blacks are discriminated against; women are prostituted; and huge numbers of Chicanos, Puerto Ricans, and other Latin Americans are scorned, exploited, and humiliated, speak of human rights?

"How can the representatives of a capitalist and imperialist society based on the exploitation of man by man, combined with egoism, individualism, and a complete lack of human solidarity, do this?

"How can those that train and provide military supplies to the bloodiest, most reactionary, and most corrupt governments in the world, such as those of Somoza, Pinochet, Stroessner, the gorillas in Uruguay, Mobutu, and the shah of Iran, just to name a few, mouth this slogan?

"How can the leaders of a state whose intelligence agencies organized assassination attempts against the leaders of other countries and whose armies dropped explosives in Vietnam equivalent to hundreds of atom bombs, such as those that exploded over Hiroshima and Nagasaki, and who murdered millions of Vietnamese without even deigning to apologize to the country or pay indemnity for the lives lost – the leaders of a state that has traditionally intervened in Latin America, subjects the people of this part of the world to its exploiting yoke, and is responsible for the deaths of hundreds of children every year due to illness and starvation – how can they speak of human rights?

"In short, how can the imperialist government that forcibly maintains a military base in our territory and subjects our people to a criminal economic blockade speak of human rights?"

The truth is that the revolution has greatly improved and extended human rights to all Cubans.

Illiteracy, which before the revolution affected almost half of the population, has been eliminated, and all Cubans are now guaranteed free education through college. Cuba has one of the highest rates of people enrolled in classes in the entire world.

After the revolution, an entirely free health care system was created, and it has become by far the best of any underdeveloped country in the world. The average life expectancy in Cuba has risen from fifty-nine years to over seventy-five. In fact, the infant mortality rate – that is the number of children that die in their first year of life – is lower in Cuba than in the United States!

A Cuban woman explains what this has meant for her

124

family, "Since the revolution, we have national healthcare. The revolution brought that, and gave my mother two life saving operations. Two. That would not have been possible before the revolution. Not at all. Without the revolution, my mother would be dead by now."

As a part of its internationalist policy, Cuba has sent thousands of volunteer doctors and nurses to countries all around the world.

While the other countries of Latin America face chronic unemployment, with rates up to fifty percent, this problem no longer exists in Cuba.

Prior to 1959, the only "jobs" available to women were those of domestic servant and prostitute – Cuba was even known as the "sleeperhouse of the Caribbean." Since the revolution those "jobs" have been all but completely eliminated, while an continually increasing number of women are entering into the labor force in all fields or taking up positions in government. Cuba has the world's most advanced system of benefits for mothers-to-be, and free birth control and abortion has been made available to all women. Also, Cuban women are guaranteed a living wage whether they work or not, so they do not have to marry or remain married out of financial considerations.

In Cuba, whether a couple or not, both parents are obligated to support their children. No child is considered illegitimate, and both men and women are responsible for the maintenance of the home.

In 1958, 75 percent of the land was controlled by 8 percent of the property owners. Following the victory of the revolution, one of the most extensive and wide ranging land reforms in the world was undertaken, bringing immensely better living conditions and opportunities to the country's many farmers and agricultural workers.

Before the revolution Blacks and Mulattos faced severe

125

discrimination, and in fact, in the island nation, Blacks weren't even allowed to go to the beach! After the revolution discrimination was wiped out, and pride in Cuba's African heritage has been continually increasing ever since.

As Eric, a Black Cuban, explained to author C. Peter Ripley, "Our life here before the revolution was a lot like in the United States I think. Maybe worse, I don't know. But I know what the revolution has meant for people like me. There was prejudice. It was very bad, to be Black. To be Black and poor. It was very bad. We could do nothing. I wish my English was better so I could explain better.

"Now we can do whatever everyone else can. Be here or there. Hold important jobs. When people in the United States talk about Cuba, there never ask people like me what I think, what we think.

"We will never go back to the way things were. We can't. Won't."

Democracy and Freedom of Speech

A long standing myth, promoted by the U.S. government and enemies of the revolution, is that democracy doesn't exist in Cuba. In fact, Cuba has one of the most democratic systems in the world!

Cubans select their representatives through a process known as Poder Popular (Peoples Power) in elections that take place every 2.5 years.

Cubans sixteen and older elect, via direct and secret ballot, city and provincial leaders, and representatives of the National Assembly. The National Assembly in turn nominates and then elects the president.

But what is it that makes Cuba's system so democratic

First of all, the Cuban people themselves meet and

126

nominate candidates, and anyone can be selected, including non-members of the PCC (Cuban Communist Party). Most who are selected are workers or peasants, or students who are children of workers or peasants. As Ricardo Alarcón, president of Cuba's parliament explains, "In other words, everyone within society can nominate whoever they want, and then make up their own minds." Tellingly, although the PCC presents no lists or candidates, over three quarters of successful candidates are party members.

Secondly, campaigns – which in capitalist "democracies" consist of rich politicians and their friends spending huge sums of money on television, radio, and newspaper ads in which they deceive voters with false promises – are a thing of the past in Cuba. Instead, a resume of each candidate, including a photograph and a biography listing things such as education and experience are posted in public places prior to the election.

Finally, all representatives are subject to recall by their electors. In other words, if the people are not satisfied with their representatives, they can vote to remove them from their position, and then nominate and elect someone else to replace them.

This truly democratic process, completely impartial and free from corruption, explains why elections in Cuba have voter turnouts of 95 percent and higher, while in "democratic" capitalist countries like the U.S. less than half of the eligible voters ever cast a ballot.

It doesn't end there. The Cuban people are involved in all aspects of society through their work places and unions, and mass organizations like the Federation of Cuban Women and Committees in Defense of the Revolution. Delegates of Peoples Power meet with those they represent on a regular basis, not only discussing their problems, but offering solutions. In Cuba, even congressional bills and laws are submitted to the people for their discussion and approval!

127

And as anyone that has visited Cuba will tell you, Cubans who are critical of the government have no fear in voicing their views.

The truth is, the revolution could not have lasted over forty-six years, under continual attack, were it not for the full support of the Cuban people, because, after all, the revolution is the Cuban people.

The Revolution Continues

To be sure, life in Cuba is not perfect. Through all the shortages and crises (many of which were created by the U.S. government in one way or another), the leadership of the revolution has always been completely honest with the Cuban people.

A fair comparison between the conditions US and Cuba can't me made, because they are very different countries with extremely different social systems. The United States is a giant capitalist, imperialist country which exploits and invades other, weaker countries for material goods (such as oil), cheap labor, and markets to sell its goods, while Cuba is a small socialist nation, which according to its own principles can only acquire foreign goods by dealing fairly with other countries, even when they don't want to deal fairly with Cuba. But comparing Cuba with other underdeveloped, former colonies with similar histories helps put the accomplishments of the revolution in perspective.

The revolution has not made every Cuban rich, giving them each a car and a houseboat, nor have any of its leaders ever claimed that it would. Cuba was a poor country before the revolution, and will most likely continue to be (as will the other underdeveloped countries of the world) until a more just, socialist social order is established in a substantial part of the world. This social order will be established when the working class and oppressed people of other countries come together and carry out their own socialist revolutions.

What the revolution has done however, in the face of ongoing attacks and a criminal economic blockade by the most powerful nation in the world, is provide completely free healthcare and education to all, eliminate illiteracy, take the land and houses of the rich and redistribute them to make sure everyone has a place to live, put all businesses and industry in the hands of the Cuban people, end racial discrimination, end the exploitation and discrimination of women, provided thousands of doctors and other volunteers to poor, underdeveloped countries around the world, and most importantly, it has done away with the exploiters, the rich parasites that make enormous amounts of money by exploiting the work of the vast majority of people (the working class) in capitalist countries like the U.S.

A young Cuban explains, "I think some people come to Cuba to find our unhappiness. They can only see what we don't have. The things that make life in Cuba different from the States, as if there's only one way to make happiness."

He continues, "I have one friend who went to Miami. He came back for a visit, and once he got to Havana, he refused to leave. He told me that in America he knew no one. No one spoke to him. No one looked him in the eyes when he walked on the sidewalk. He was really unhappy. Told me that drugs and violence and racism scared him, a lot."

Since 1959 the Cuban people have been building their own society, a socialist society based on solidarity, real democracy, justice, and equality, and they will continue to do so no matter what the obstacle, as Che said, "Hasta la victoria, siempre (until the victory, always)!"

Celebrate genocide? No thanks!

On November 24, many in the U.S. gathered with their families to feast in (unintentional?) celebration of the worst genocide in human history.

Taught from childhood that the friendly Pilgrims invited the Indians to a great feast after surviving their first year in New England, little do most of them know that the real history of Thanksgiving is a story of mass murder and theft.

The Real Story Of Thanksgiving

For the entire story, we could go back to the first landing of Columbus in what is now the Dominican Republic in 1942; but being as though that is outside of the scope of this article, we'll focus on the events in North America that lead to the creation of the modern day Thanksgiving holiday.

In 1614 a small group of English explorers sailed home from North America with a ship full of Patuxet Indians that were to be used as slaves. Those who escaped capture were virtually wiped out by the smallpox they had left behind.

One of the original colonists would later describe the mass deaths as a gift from God, writing "But for the natives in these parts, God hath so pursued them, as for 300 miles space the greatest part of them are swept away by smallpox which still continues among them. So as God hath thereby cleared our title to this place."

By the time the group of religious zealots, called Puritans, arrived in Massachusetts Bay four years later, they found only one Patuxet survivor, a man named Squanto who had survived slavery in Europe and spoke the colonists' language. He taught them how to plant corn and catch fish and helped negotiate a peace treaty with the nearby Wampanoag Nation. This enabled the Puritans to survive their first year in

North America, quite a feat considering that previous settlements like those in Virginia had been completely wiped out in a few months time. At the end of the year they held a great feast honoring Squanto and the Wampanoags.

As word spread throughout England about the paradise to the west, religious exiles began heading to the "new world" by the boat load. They began discussing who exactly owned the land they had settled on. Their method of farming was based on individual ownership, as opposed to the Indians who practiced communal farming, and to whom land "ownership" was a completely alien idea.

A few of the Puritans argued that the land belonged to the Indians that inhabited it, but they were soon expelled from the settlements. Governor Winthrop of Massachusetts declared that since the Indians had not fenced in and cultivated all of the land, it was public domain, which under English Common Law meant that it belonged to the King. So then, it was decided that the local governor, not the Indians, would decide what would be done with the land.

The settlers then joined up in groups and seized vast stretches of land, captured strong young Natives for slaves to work it, and killed old men, women, and children for whom they had no use.

The Pequot Nation, who had never agreed to the peace treaty negotiated by Squanto, fought back. The war between the Pequot and English would be one of the bloodiest in North America.

In 1637 over 700 men, women, and children gathered near present day Groton, Connecticut to celebrate their annual Green Corn Festival. But early that morning they were surrounded by English and Dutch mercenaries who ordered them to come outside. Those who did were shot or beaten to death while the terror-stricken women and children who hid inside the longhouse were burned alive.

The governor of Plymouth wrote about the events, "Those that escaped the fire were slain with the sword; some hewed to pieces, others run through with their rapiers, so that they were quickly dispatched and very few escaped. It was conceived they thus destroyed about 400 at this time. It was a fearful sight to see them thus frying in the fire...horrible was the stink and scent thereof, but the victory seemed a sweet sacrifice, and they gave the prayers thereof to God, who had wrought so wonderfully for them."

The next day, the governor of the Massachusetts Bay Colony declared "A Day of Thanksgiving" for the massacre.

From then on, the colonists waged a vicious campaign against the Indians, attacking village after village. Women and children over 14 were captured and sold into slavery while the others were murdered. Boats full of "human cargo" regularly shipped out from the ports of New England. After discovering just how profitable the slave trade could be, the burgeoning capitalists would go on to enslave millions of Africans and Asians.

"Scalp bounties" were offered for Indian scalps by the local governments to encourage as many murders as possible.

Another "Day of Thanksgiving" was proclaimed in the churches of Manhattan after a mercenary hired by the governor set a village of hundreds of Indians of fire near what is now Stamford, Connecticut.

The killings continued to increase, and "day of thanksgiving" feasts were held after each successful slaughter. After a few years, there were almost no Indians left in the Northern English colonies.

George Washing finally suggested that one day of Thanksgiving be held per year, instead of celebrating each bloodbath individually. Later, President Lincoln would declare Thanksgiving Day to be a legal holiday during the civil war.

Since the first landing of Europeans in the Americas,

hundreds of millions of human beings have been killed. Thanksgiving has been celebrated annually in the United States since 1863.

A Day Of Mourning

The state of Massachusetts invited Wamsutta of the Wampanoag to give a speech during their 350th anniversary celebration of thanksgiving in 1970. However, when the planners reviewed his speech beforehand, they wouldn't allow it and instead wrote an alternative speech. Wamsutta refused to give the speech written by the planners and instead, to protest the continued silencing of the American Indians, he and his supporters went to neighboring Coles Hill. Overlooking the Plymouth Harbor and the Mayflower replica, Wamsutta gave his original speech.

In it he said, "Today is a time of celebrating for you -- a time of looking back to the first days of white people in America. But it is not a time of celebrating for me. It is with a heavy heart that I look back upon what happened to my people. When the Pilgrims arrived, we, the Wampanoags, welcomed them with open arms, little knowing that it was the beginning of the end. That before 50 years were to pass, the Wampanoag would no longer be a tribe. That we and other Indians living near the settlers would be killed by their guns or dead from diseases that we caught from them.

"History wants us to believe that the Indian was a savage, illiterate, uncivilized animal. A history that was written by an organized, disciplined people, to expose us as an unorganized and undisciplined entity. Two distinctly different cultures met. One thought they must control life; the other believed life was to be enjoyed, because nature decreed it. Let us remember, the Indian is and was just as human as the white man."

This marked the first National Day of Mourning.

The few Americans Indians that survived the 500 year genocide are the poorest ethnic group in the richest country in the world. Each year, a group of them, along with supporters of all shades, gather at Plymouth Rock on Thanksgiving Day for a day of mourning, during which they fast, remember what is lost, and protest against continued racism and injustice.

"Some ask us: Will you ever stop protesting?" said Moonanum James in a speech on the 29th National Day of Mourning in 1998. "Some day we will stop protesting: We will stop protesting when the merchants of Plymouth are no longer making millions of dollars off the blood of our slaughtered ancestors. We will stop protesting when we can act as sovereign nations on our own land without the interference of the Bureau of Indian Affairs and what Sitting Bull called the "favorite ration chiefs." When corporations stop polluting our mother, the earth. When racism has been eradicated. When the oppression of Two-Spirited people is a thing of the past. We will stop protesting when homeless people have homes and no child goes to bed hungry. When police brutality no longer exists in communities of color. We will stop protesting when Leonard Peltier and Mumia Abu Jamal and the Puerto Rican independentistas and all the political prisoners are free.

"Until then, the struggle will continue."

Columbus day? There's nothing to celebrate!

On October 12th many Americans, especially students in first and secondary schools, will celebrate "Columbus Day." They will be bombarded with propaganda describing Columbus as a "great explorer" who "discovered" America.

The truth of course, is that the Americas were already discovered over 10,000 years earlier by the ancestors of the people that inhabited it when Columbus landed.

It has also been claimed that Europeans believed the Earth was flat, and that Columbus proved them wrong. This myth can be traced back to Washington Irving's novel *The Life and Voyages of Christopher Columbus* (1828).

The fact that the Earth is round was evident to most people of Columbus's time, especially other sailors and explorers (Eratosthenes (276-194 BC) had in fact accurately calculated the circumference of the Earth). The only thing in dispute was the distance to the Indies (where Columbus planned to sail).

Most European sailors and navigators concluded that the Indies were too far away to make sailing to them worth considering. They were right and Columbus was wrong; had he not unexpectedly encountered a previously uncharted continent in mid-travel, he and his crew would have perished from lack of food and water.

So it was that Columbus and his crew landed on what is now the Dominican Republic in 1492, encountering the Islands original inhabitants, the Tainos. Columbus himself described them; "These people have no religious beliefs, nor are they idolaters. They are very gentle and do not know what evil is; nor do they kill others, nor steal; and they are without weapons."

After sailing along the northern coasts of the Island of Hispaniola and Cuba (where he viewed mountains that he thought were the Himalayas in India), Columbus proceeded to kidnap several Tainos and steal gold and other resources to display on his return to Spain.

On his second voyage, Columbus took 1600 Arawak (inhabitants of Cuba) as slaves and imposed a brutal system on the natives in Haiti, whereby all those above fourteen years of age had to find a certain quota of gold, or, if they failed, have their hands chopped off.

Columbus was a mad man who claimed that God spoke to him, lobbied for a new crusade to Jerusalem, and described his explorations to to "paradise" as a part of God's plan which would soon result in the Last Judgment and the end of the world.

But the worst had yet to come. European expansion into the Americas eventually resulted in the deaths of millions of indigenous people.

As David E. Stannard, a historian at the University of Hawaii, puts it, "[the indigenous people had undergone the] worst human holocaust the world had ever witnessed, roaring across two continents non-stop for four centuries and consuming the lives of countless tens of millions of people."

In 1989, former U.S. president George Bush I said that "[Columbus] set an example for us all by showing what monumental feats can be accomplished through perseverance and faith." This, which was said in reference to a man who founded the Atlantic slave trade in which millions of Africans were transferred across the Atlantic for sale as slaves and initiated genocide against the indigenous people of the Americas, reveals perfectly the intentions of the U.S. imperialism.

On the other hand, in October of 2002, Venezuelan President Hugo Chavez signed a decree changing the name of the country's "Columbus Day" to "The Day of Indigenous Resistance" in honor of the nation's indigenous groups. On October 12, 2004, after finding him guilty of "imperialist genocide," a group of Venezuelans destroyed a 100-year old statue of Columbus in the capital city of Caracas.

And rightly so! Instead of being celebrated with a holiday, the atrocities of Columbus and those like him should be roundly condemned by all.

Hugo Chavez, Venezuela and the Bolivarian Revolution

Venezuelan President Hugo Chavez Speaks

Fresh from a day spent visiting the "Point Community Development Corporation" in New York's South Bronx neighborhood where he met with the leaders of dozens of social groups and residents of the Bronx, Venezuelan President Hugo Chavez entered the packed Church of St. Paul and St. Andrew in Manhattan on the night of Saturday, September 17 to a standing ovation and chants of "Chavez, Chavez!" The large crowd had waited hours to hear the president speak.

President Chavez began the speech in English, using a few basic phrases he learned in school and bringing laughter to the crowd. He went on to tell the audience that rather than them thank him for coming, he should thank them for coming to listen.

He then greeted some special guests in attendance including the Reverend Jesse Jackson, U.S. Congressman Jose Serrano, Fr. Roy Bourgeois - founder of the School of the Americas Watch, the president of Pastors for Peace, actor Danny Glover, president of the National Assembly of Peoples Power of Cuba Ricardo Alarcon, and many others.

After thanking the president of the local transportation union, President Chavez continued by announcing that Venezuela, an oil producing country where gasoline is sold for fifteen cents a gallon thanks to government policies, was reiterating its offer of low cost gasoline (through it's company CITGO), heating oil, and fuel to generate energy to poor communities, hospitals, universities, churches, and others in the U.S. He said that the current price for heating oil in the U.S. was around three dollars a gallon. "This is a bit high I think."

He advised the people in attendance that Venezuela could offer heating oil, gasoline and fuel at very low prices, as long as there were no middle men. Other deals could be made, he said, such as long term loans at the lowest possible rates, and grants to universities and hospitals.

The president then assured the audience that he had no hard feelings towards the American people. He said that his criticisms of the Bush administration, usually made in retaliation to verbal attacks against him by U.S. officials, were sometimes misconstrued as attacks against the American people. "I love the people of the United States," he said.

Speaking on the U.S. invasion and occupation of Iraq, Chavez said it was justifiable for people in an invaded country to defend themselves. "The true war we ask for is the war against poverty and misery," he said, drawing an extended applause from the audience.

Chavez explained Venezuela's recent efforts to clean up their rivers, and said he had advised the president of Venezuelan owned CITGO to hire environmental experts to study the Bronx river in order to find out what would be necessary to clean it as well. He said Venezuela would fund the undertaking, as long as the U.S. government didn't object.

President Chavez reiterated the generous offers of both his country and Cuba to aid victims of Hurricane Katrina, to which the U.S. government have still not responded. The two countries were among the first in the world to offer aid. "Cuba had two thousand doctors ready to go ... they are only two hours away," he said. "The generators are still in the airplanes [waiting to go]."

The president explained that when it was originally thought that Hurricane Katrina would strike Havana, the capital city of Cuba, 2,000,000 people, along with their pets and all farm animals in danger, were safely evacuated. He pointed to this as a model for others.

When he informed the audience that Fidel Castro was listening to the speech from Cuba, the crowd immediately rose to their feet and gave a rousing applause. Chants of "Viva Fidel!" and "Viva Cuba!" echoed throughout the church.

Chavez spoke shortly about the speech he had given two days earlier at the United Nations summit. The speech, in which he delivered a fiery criticism of U.S. President Bush, capitalism, and American imperialism, and proposed moving the UN to a city in the developing world, drew the loudest and most enthusiastic applause at the summit. Cuban leaders Fidel Castro and Ernesto 'Che' Guevara drew similar responses after their historic debut addresses before the general assembly in the 1960's.

President Chavez then explained to the audience the reasoning behind Venezuela and Cuba's choice to register protest to the 35-page agreement that came out of the summit. He said the two countries were excluded from the final drafting of the deal, and singled out one issue in particular. A section of the document apparently outlined a "responsibility to protect." "Is that what they're doing in Iraq now, protecting?" he asked. "Tomorrow or sometime in the future, someone in Washington will say that the Venezuelan people need to be protected from the tyrant Chavez, who is a threat."

Towards the end of the speech, the Venezuelan president extended an offer from his people, and the people of Cuba, to treat Americans with eye problems that were unable to afford the necessary treatment. "Between 80,000 and 100,000 a year" would be treated he said, as a part of a total of 6 million patients from around the world who will be treated over the next ten years. He said the government of Venezuela would pay all related expenses, including transportation to and from the United States, and that any interested parties should contact the Venezuelan consulate.

The Americans would be flown to Caracas, explained Chavez, where some of them would remain to receive treatment, but most would continue on to Havana via one of three Venezuelan airplanes since Cuba is equipped to treat more patients.

Cuba's completely free medical system is world renowned, and Cuban doctors have been treating patients from around the world for decades, both within Cuba and abroad. Most of them would not have received health care otherwise.

According to Chavez, 20,000 Cuban doctors are currently in Venezuela, training local doctors and treating patients, and 90,000 Venezuelans have received medical treatment in Cuba this year alone. "Our goal is 100,000," he said. This is treatment they wouldn't have been able to receive in their own country, because Venezuela, like many countries, doesn't have the advanced equipment needed for certain operations. The president said they were making strides towards getting such equipment.

Chavez also told the story of his own daughter, who had recently had foot and eye problems diagnosed and then treated in Cuba. Cuban doctors successfully operated on a congenial cataract in her eyes and a tendon in her foot. "She says she can run a little bit faster now," he said, drawing laughter from the audience.

Before ending, Chavez told the crowd that Venezuela has the largest oil reserves in the world, as well as sizable gas deposits, and that they wanted to share them with everyone. The president brought the speech to a close amid a standing ovation with the immortal words of the revolutionary Ernesto 'Che' Guevara, *"Hasta la victoria, siempre (ever onward to victory)!"*

Venezuela's Elections and Washington's Dirty Tricks

Venezuela's capitalist class and it's supporters in the U.S. Government did all they could to sabotage the recent legislative elections in Venezuela; the latest in a series of attempts to overthrow democratically elected President Hugo Chavez (including a coup in April 2002 that was defeated by a popular uprising, an industry shutdown by the oil bosses in 2002-2003, and a 2004 referendum), but they failed again.

As polls indicated that a coalition of parties lead by Chavez's Fifth Republic Movement (MVR) would easily gain a majority in the legislature, the two main capitalist parties -- Accion Democratica and COPEI -- that took turns ruling Venezuela for the last four decades, chose to boycott the scheduled elections days before they occurred. They spuriously claimed that the voting machines in use could not be trusted, even though international observers have said the machines are far more reliable than most of those used in the US 2004 elections.

In an effort to compromise, election officials even agreed to remove the machines and instead use paper ballots, but the capitalist parties boycotted anyway.

It just a part of their ongoing campaign, which is receiving strong backing from corporate media in Venezuela and abroad, to discredit the electoral system and paint Chavez as a "dictator", paving the way for them to call for U.S. intervention.

The boycott was lead by Sumate, a group funded by the U.S. National Endowment for Democracy (NED), which is infamous for interfering in the political processes of other countries and funding the election campaigns of candidates friendly to American businessmen. In 2004 the NED brought in $80.1 million dollars, $79.25 of which came directly from the U.S. Government. Of course, the U.S. lends political as well as economical support. In fact, Maria Corina Machado, the leader of Sumate, just met with George W. Bush in the White House six months before the elections occurred.

And, as if a boycott wasn't enough, the capitalist and imperialist team also planned for violence.

142

Thankfully, Venezuelan security forces were able to foil a CIA-backed plot by a small band of active and former army officers and mercenaries to attack military bases and assassinate government officials in order to destabilize the country and force the elections to be suspended. But not all parts of the plan were stopped. A key oil pipeline was blown up with C-4 explosives the night before the elections, two fragmentation grenades exploded at a Caracas army base, and three people were injured when a pipe bomb exploded at a government office.

A day earlier, Venezuelan military officials discovered stockpiles of guns, grenades, and another 24 pounds of C-4 in the northeastern state of Zulia.

"They wanted to suspend the elections, attack the president and kill key government leaders," Nicolas Maduro, President of the National Assembly, told a news conference.

"The opposition are just a bunch of thieves who tried to sabotage the election," pensioner Pedro Zamora, who was voting in eastern Chacao district, told reporters. "We can see the government are going to get most of the votes."

Three Venezuelan lawmakers presented a recording involving active and retired dissident military officers talking about causing 15,000 deaths, chaos, and attacks on government institutions.

"The CIA is behind this plan," said Celia Flores, one of the lawmakers.

"Undoubtedly we are in the presence of a superior body that is in charge of concocting all of these actions and which will benefit from the deaths of thousands of Venezuelans," added Pedro Carreño, Vice President of the National Assembly. "[They] are not mistaken when they say that behind this is the CIA."

The Votes Are In

When all was said and done, the MVR and its allies swept the elections, picking up all 167 seats in the National Assembly. But in part because of the boycott, bombing, and torrential rains that occurred the day of the election, a large percentage of Venezuela's electorate chose to stay home, with about 25% voting.

Right on cue, the U.S. Government was their to condemn the elections.

"The abstention rate was very high," said State Department spokesman Adam Ereli. "Given that rate of abstention, plus expressions of concern by prominent [read: rich] Venezuelans, we would see that this reflects a broad lack of confidence in the impartiality and transparency of the electoral process."

The capitalist parties did the same, attempting to paint the newly elected National Assembly as an "illegitimate body".

The truth however, is that the new assembly is just as legitimate as any that came before it. As Interior Minister Jesse Chacon pointed out in a press conference, in the 1998 elections, Accion Democratica won control of the National Assembly with the support of just 11.24 percent of registered voters, which is less than half the percentage (of a much larger electorate) the MVR-led coalition won in the latest election. Furthermore, only 10% of the 5,000 some candidates actually pulled out of the elections.

And, as Venezuelan Vice President José Vicente Rangel pointed out, "There are countries like the US in which only 25 percent participate in the elections to Congress". Washington doesn't raise questions about the legitimacy of those elections.

Lastly, hundreds of international observers from the European Union and the Organization of American States called the elections "transparent and fair",

144

At A Crossroads

This just the latest attempt in an ongoing campaign by Venezuela's capitalist class -- and it's imperialist backers in the U.S. -- to overthrow the democratically elected Chavez, overturn the processes taking place, and reinstate their neo-liberal system.

But this, like the 2004 referendum that confirmed to the whole world the popular support enjoyed by Chavez, may actually serve to pave the way for a more revolutionary path to be taken up by the Venezuelan people.

The National Assembly has spoke of amending the constitution to remove the limit of two presidential terms in office, which would allow Chavez to seek a third term in 2006. All indications are that he would be elected by a landslide, as no formidable opponents have emerged.

This -- accompanied with an increased effort to arm workers and their allies and the formation of more workers' councils -- would be a positive step Venezuela's unfolding process.

Workers and other oppressed people must also step up efforts to organize and mobilize in defense of Venezuela. We must unite around the demand: Hands off Venezuela!

Venezuela assists poor Americans with heating oil

Venezuelan humanitarian aid has arrived in New York and Massachusetts as promised by President Hugo Chavez months earlier.

At a time when U.S. oil companies have refused to lower prices and Congress has failed to deliver aid in response to rising oil prices, thousands of poor residents of

Massachusetts and the Bronx are receiving low cost heating oil to help them make it through the winter.

The assistance was welcome in the Mount Hood neighborhood of the Bronx, where "we accept food stamps" signs fill supermarket windows and dreary housing projects fill the skyline.

"It's very hard as a single parent, trying to raise a child, and on welfare. I'm just trying to manage," said Bronx resident Yolanda Ayabarreno at an event to announce the delivery.

Congressman Jose Serrano, who helped the Venezuelan government put the program together, said he was trying the best he could for the Bronx.

"To those folks who say that this is a way for Hugo Chavez to score political points, I invite every American corporation that wants to score points with my community, to start scoring points this afternoon," he said.

Citgo, the U.S. arm of the Venezuelan state oil company, will deliver another 20 million gallons of heating oil this winter to tens of thousands of New York and Massachusetts families at steep discounts.

So, while the U.S. government has done nothing to alleviate the impact record oil prices are having on its own poor, Venezuela is offering them tens of millions of dollars in assistance.

"The federal government of the United States makes billions off the high price of crude oil and yet they haven't increased the amount of fuel assistance one dime despite the fact that the price of oil has nearly doubled in the past two years," said Joe Kennedy, chairman of Citizens Energy, one of the organizations that will distribute the oil.

Venezuela is "the one country that has agreed to provide our poor people with some low-cost oil and it's the country that gets the greatest amount of criticism," he said.

Bolivia: A Revolution Betrayed, Again

A revolution betrayed, again

For weeks throughout May and June, angry miners and factory workers, joined by peasants, Indians, teachers, students, organizations of the unemployed, thousands of slum dwellers from the impoverished city of El Alto and tens of thousands of others poured into the capital city of La Paz, demanding "Nationalization of gas and oil," and "Obreros al poder" (workers to power).

In the face of government threats of violence, protestors occupied several oil facilities while peasants cut off the river which supplies water to La Paz.

Indian women, armed with sticks and pieces of wood, forced shops and street merchants to close.

Miners exploded dynamite and riot police fired tear gas as demonstrators fought to break police lines and seize central La Paz to shut down the Bolivian Congress.

An unlimited strike was called and protestors successfully blockaded key supply routes making it impossible to for delivery trucks to enter the city.

The protests began after a hydrocarbons law that guaranteed imperialist "multinational" energy corporations' (Enron, British Petroleum, Shell, etc) profits was passed by the Bolivian Congress and signed by right-wing Santa Cruz senator Hormando Vaca Diez (fearing the reaction of the masses, Mesa didn't sign the law himself). The reaction was immediate and Congress and Mesa fled the capital.

The oppressed people of Bolivia were fighting for the immediate aim of the nationalization of the abundant gas and oil reserves in their country. "Multinational" corporations exploit these abundant resources to reap huge profits, while Bolivia remains the poorest country in South America, with a per capita GDP of a mere $2,600.

But nationalizations are not enough to solve Bolivia's deep rooted problems, and many, if not most of its oppressed people know this.

The uprising was also driven by the call from the rich, and openly racist, bourgeoisie of the gas-producing eastern Santa Cruz de la Sierra department and southern Tarija department (which are also the "whitest" regions in a country with an Indian majority) for "autonomy," guaranteeing them even more wealth while keeping out the Indian masses of the highlands.

Evo Morales, leader of the Movement Towards Socialism (MAS-Movimiento al Socialismo), was largely seen as the "leader" of the protestors, though, after his failed attempts to limit the activity of the protestors, he himself admitted, "the rank and file have outflanked us." Morales received the support of most of the Bolivian labor, union, peasant and Indian leaders, and has even been lauded by some so-called "leftists" as a "revolutionary," though in reality he is no more than a parliamentary reformist.

Deja Vu

The events are a continuation of the 2003 "gas war" in Bolivia. Following his failed attempt to crush a demonstration -- against his attempted deals with "multinational" gas corporations -- with ruthless repression, then-president, and Washington favorite, Gonzalo Sanchez de Lozada ("Goni") was forced from power by a worker and Indian uprising.

Following his ouster, the armed forces and Bolivian Government, with the blessings of the U.S. embassy, gave power to Goni's vice-president, former journalist Carlos Mesa.

Leaders of the workers, peasants, Indians and others

involved in the 2003 uprising took the reformist road, deciding to "give Mesa a chance." Anyone with a proper understanding of the situation of course, saw it then as the defeat it was.

While Mesa, in an attempt to subdue the angry oppressed masses, promised reform soon after gaining power, the reality of his rule was much different. The unelected president served no one but the imperialist "multinational" corporations and the United States government. One of his moves in office was convincing the Bolivian Senate to grant immunity from the law for U.S. troops.

Mesa also played into the interests of the racist right-wing bourgeoisie in the richest regions of the country, granting them elections for departmental governors (to occur in August), to which they opportunistically attached an "autonomy" referendum.

In March, Mesa claimed he was resigning in protest to the "crazy" demands of labor, Indian and peasant groups, only to reverse his decision and vow to stay in office for the duration of his term (until 2007).

But after weeks of protests and blockades, and in the face of very real threats of a military coup, Mesa had no choice but to finally submit his resignation in early June. He was replaced by a "caretaker" president, Eduardo Rodriguez, by the Bolivian Congress.

Compromise Spells Defeat

At a crucial time when the Bolivian ruling class was divided and weak, and the working class had its best opportunity yet to seize power, the leaders of the workers, Indian and other groups called and end to the protests and blockades following an agreement by Rodriguez to hold early elections.

The reformist Morales declared a "truce," conveniently

paving the way for his candidacy in the early elections which Rodriguez must arrange within five months. Once again the workers, Indians and the rest of the oppressed masses of Bolivia have been sold out by their "leadership."

But the conditions that created this uprising -- and that of 2003 -- have not gone away; and, as at the conclusion of that 2003 uprising, the oppressed Bolivian people are not defeated.

"Our life is very sad. We have carpenters and day laborers who can't find work, the children go hungry and sometimes all you eat in a day is a bowl of watery soup ... and look at the politicians who keep all our money and have gardeners and maids," said Carmela de Nina, 67. "We are lifting the blockades for now, but this can start again at any time."

The working people, peasants, Indians and other oppressed Bolivian people must organize and fight for their interests collectively under the leadership of the working class, not settling for a reformist "truce" or simple nationalization. In order to solve the problems of centuries of poverty and exploitation, and to break free from the clutches of imperialism, they must wrestle the power from the hands of the ruling class through a genuine socialist revolution, and establish a state in which they have the power!

Is Fidel Castro one of the richest men in the world?

In 2005, American business and financial magazine *Forbes* listed Castro among the world's richest people, with an estimated net worth of $550 million. The estimates claimed that the Cuban leader's personal wealth was nearly double that of Britain's Queen Elizabeth II, despite evidence from diplomats and businessmen that the Cuban leader's personal life was notably austere. *Forbes* later increased the estimates to $900 million, adding rumors of large cash stashes in Switzerland. The magazine offered no proof at all of this information.

Of course it was all entirely bogus – the bunk methodology they used was based on the lie that Fidel Castro owns everything in the entire country of Cuba. Even in their article they admitted their "estimate" was "more art than science" — or in other words, bullshit.

Fidel's response?

"PRESIDENT Fidel Castro has challenged and called on Bush, the CIA, the 33 U.S. intelligence agencies, the thousands of banks in the world and the 'servants' of *Forbes* magazine, which claims that Fidel has a fortune of $900 million, to prove that he has even one dollar in an overseas account.

"In exchange for just one shred of evidence, he said that he would offer them everything that they have tried and failed to do over almost half a century, during which time they have tried to destroy the Revolution and assassinate him via hundreds of conspiracies. 'I'm giving you everything you've tried,' he said, 'and don't come with your foolishness and wayside stories. Show me an account, of just one dollar,'" he emphasized.

"If they can prove that I have one single dollar, I will resign from all my responsibilities and the duties I am carrying out; they won't need any more plans or transitions, if they can prove that I have one single dollar," the revolutionary leader said emphatically." – *Granma* newspaper

Later:

"Bush has not uttered a word and neither have the State Department, Congress or the CIA. Only the *Nuevo Herald*, a Miami newspaper, has tried to defend [the Forbes article] at the request of the Cuban-American mafia [the handful of rich white Cubans who left the country after the revolution because they didn't want to be equal with the rest of the people]. This silence by the US Administration demonstrates the extent of its weakness." – Radio Habana

Even the *Miami Herald*, a rightwing newspaper with ties to the Cuban-American mafia that is historically hostile to the Cuban Revolution admits that Fidel Castro lives in about the same conditions as everyone else in Cuba. The newspaper has previously printed articles in which it acknowledges that:

"The houses of Fidel and Raúl are large but simply appointed.... The living room of [Fidel's] house is described by visitors as furnished with simple wood and leather sofas and chairs and Cuban handicrafts.... The only luxury visible to visitors is a big-screen television...."

Was there a split between Che Guevara and Fidel Castro?

A rumor persists to this day that Ernesto 'Che' Guevara and Fidel Castro had some sort of falling out near the end of Che's life that caused him to leave Cuba and prompted Fidel to withhold support for the guerrilla effort Che lead in Bolivia. But with a little investigation, we find that there is no evidence whatsoever to support this rumor, which, it should be noted, originated with Felix Rodriguez, a wealthy Cuban-born CIA assassin who ordered Che's murder.

And what is the supposed source of major disagreement between Che and Fidel? Some have suggested that Che was critical of the USSR. A review of Fidel Castro's speeches in the 1960's, in which he criticized the USSR several times, easily dispels that myth. Still others have claimed that Che took the side of China while Fidel took the side of the USSR in the Sino-Soviet Split. This too, is easily disproven.

Che wrote that:

"When we analyze the lonely situation of the Vietnamese people, we are overcome by anguish at this illogical moment of humanity.

"U.S. imperialism is guilty of aggression — its crimes are enormous and cover the whole world. We already know all that, gentlemen! But this guilt also applies to those who, when the time came for a definition, hesitated to make Vietnam an inviolable part of the socialist world; running, of course, the risks of a war on a global scale-but also forcing a decision upon imperialism. And the guilt also applies to those who maintain a war of abuse and snares — started quite some time ago by the representatives of the two greatest powers of the socialist camp."[1]

While, around the same time Fidel wrote in a similar vein that:

"Without a doubt, the South Vietnamese people and the people of North Vietnam are suffering all this and suffering it in their own flesh, because there it is men and women who die, in the south and in the north, victims of the shrapnel and Yankee bombings. They do not have the slightest hesitancy in declaring that they intend to continue to carry all that out because not even the attacks against North Vietnam have resulted in overcoming the divisions in the bosom of the socialist family.

"And who can doubt that this division is encouraging the imperialists? Who can doubt that a united front against the imperialist enemy would have made them hesitate–would have made them think a little more carefully before launching their adventurist attacks and their increasingly more brazen intervention in that part of the world?"[2]

For his part, Rodriguez claimed in his autobiography that upon capture, Che "was bitter over the Cuban dictator's lack of support for the Bolivian incursion." But only a fool would believe the words of Che's enemy and murderer (who, incidentally, wears his watch to this day like a trophy). More reliable sources suggest that Che considered Rodriguez a traitor and refused to speak to him. But that hasn't stopped the capitalist press from keeping the claim alive.

As Fidel put it in a June 1987 television interview with Italian journalist Gianni Mina:

"What could we have done? Sent a battalion, a company, a regular army? The laws of guerrilla warfare are different; everything depends on what the guerrilla unit itself does."[3]

154

Che's plan to wage guerrilla war in Bolivia to initiate a socialist revolution to overthrow the dictatorship was fully supported by Cuba. Cuba provided training grounds, fighters, weapons, passports and more to the effort.

We need not pretend Che and Fidel agreed on every single question to know that there was no major disagreement that lead to abandonment or a suicidal departure.

According to the survivors of the guerrilla force he led and the pages of his personal diary, which has since been published, Che never once suggested that he felt betrayed or abandoned by Cuba or Fidel. In his farewell letter Che wrote to Fidel, "I am also proud of having followed you without hesitation, of having identified with your way of thinking and of seeing and appraising dangers and principles."

Notes
1. Guevara, Ernesto, Che. "Message to the Tricontinental."
2. Castro, Fidel. "Live speech from the steps of Havana University on the occasion of the anniversary of the attack on the Presidential Palace" (13 March 1965).
3. Mini, Gianni. "An Encounter With Fidel."

On the death of Cuban revolutionary Juan Almeida

Juan Almeida Bosque, a leader of the Cuban Revolution that toppled the bloody, U.S.-backed dictatorship of Fulgencio Batista, died at age 82.

Almeida, who was born in a poor neighborhood of Havana, Cuba, left school at age 11 to begin work in construction.

In 1952, he joined Fidel Castro and a group of young Cubans in an attack on the Moncada Military Barracks in Santiago de Cuba which was aimed at securing arms for a popular uprising against the Batista dictatorship. Many of the participants in the failed incursion were tortured and murdered. Almeida, along with Fidel Castro, Raul Castro and others, were able to escape temporarily before being apprehended.

Almeida and the other captured rebels were imprisoned on the Isle of Pines. They were freed after nearly two years in prison as a result of popular pressure.

The rebels soon after went to Mexico where they formed a guerrilla nucleus and began training for a war to overthrow Batista.

In 1956, 82 rebels set out for Cuba on a rickety yacht. Their landing, delayed and disrupted, was a disaster. Not long after touching ground, all but 16 of the guerrillas had been killed by government forces.

Almeida led a small group that included Ernesto 'Che' Guevara, the Argentine-born revolutionary who joined the Cuban revolutionaries, out into the jungle during that bleak early period.

The guerrillas were eventually able to regroup. They begun to win battles, recruit new members and supporters, establish new ties and advance.

Almeida, a crack shot, quickly became a comandante, the highest rank in the rebel army. He led one of the few guerrilla fronts during the revolutionary war.

On January 1, 1959, "Batista the Butcher" fled Cuba, realizing his overthrow was imminent. Immediately afterward, the victory of the Cuban Revolution was secured by an island-wide general strike.

The Revolution opened the doorway to equality for Almeida and other Black Cubans who previously suffered under conditions of degradation and discrimination.

Almeida held a number of positions in the revolutionary government. He was a General in the Revolutionary Armed Forces, a member of the Central Committee of the Cuban Communist Party, president of the Association of Combatants of the Revolution and Vice-President of the Cuban Council of State.

At the time of his death, Almeida was one of only three living Cubans holding the title *Commander of the Revolution.*

Almeida was also an artist and writer, having written more than 300 songs and several books on Cuban History.

Thousands of Cubans showed up at memorials across the country to bid farewell to Almeida. According to his wishes, his body is being interred at the Mausoleum of the Mario Muñoz Monroy Third Eastern Front, which he led.

A sober analysis of the writers strike in the United States

On Tuesday, February 12, 2008, the members of the Writers Guild of America voted overwhelmingly to end their 100-day-long strike.

The writers will vote to ratify a new agreement with the Alliance of Motion Picture and Television Producers (AMPTP) with mail-in ballots and at meetings held on February 25.

As bosses like the CBS Corporation's CEO Les Moonves claim "everybody won," we must make a sober analysis of the strike from the perspective of the working class.

On the one hand, the writers no doubt sent shockwaves through the industry and society at large by demonstrating such dedication in a country in which the myth of a classless "national unity" is today so prevalent.

But at the same time, the groundwork for the defeat of similar actions in the future has been laid.

Despite claims by the WGA West's lead bureaucrat Patric Verrone that "writers will lead the way as TV migrates to the internet and platforms for new media are developed," provisions in the new agreement will in fact allow "studios to hire nonunion writers to work on low-budget Internet shows," according to the *Los Angeles Times*.

The agreement also continues to exclude "reality shows" and animation from its terms, something the striking workers greatly opposed. The networks utilized such shows to continue putting new material out during the recent strike, thus undermining the writers' struggle.

A key weapon of workers in the class struggle is their ability to withdraw their labor, thus shutting down production. The above mentioned aspects of the proposed agreement greatly blunt this weapon.

The WGA leaders also gave up the writers' demands for higher revenues from DVD sales and largely gave in on the writers' demands for revenue from shows broadcast on the internet, with the new agreement guaranteeing only limited revenues to begin 17-24 days after the program is first put on the web.

The bureaucrats at the top of the WGA are pushing all of this as the living conditions of the writers continue to decline.

In a February 8 article, *Variety*, a newspaper covering the entertainment industry, pointed out "[feature film writers] have endured setbacks in virtually every area except new media in the past decade .. writers of feature films feel exploited in ways that were unthinkable 10 years ago."

And indeed, it appears the bosses largely planned out this conclusion to the strike long ago. According to an article in the *Los Angeles Times*, "WGA leaders, [FOX top Peter Chernin] told people around him, would have difficulty keeping their group united. ... The companies would be able to exploit the natural divisions within the WGA by first coming to an agreement with another union, the Directors Guild of America (DGA)."

And that is largely what happened. AMPTP reached a tentative agreement with the Directors Guild of America (whose current contract is set to expire in July) on January 17.

So, while the writers are back to work and have made some minor gains, their 100-day strike didn't go nearly far enough, and in some cases, represents a step back.

Every major poll taken during the strike showed that a vast majority of the people in the U.S. supported the writers in their struggle. An independent group calling itself "Fans4Writers" even came together, walking picket lines and bringing food to the picketers. Various unions, from the Teamsters to the SEIU, also threw their support behind the strikers (with the notable exception of Tom Short, the incredibly reactionary president of the International Alliance of Theatrical Stage Employees who condemned the writers for taking work-stop action).

This support could have been key to mobilizing thousands in support of the writers (undoubtedly to the protests of the bureaucratic union leaders who are deathly afraid of any independent action on the part of workers which could disrupt their cushy relationships with the bosses). Besides strengthening the writers in their struggle, this would have forged strong bonds of solidarity among all workers involved and strengthened the working class as a whole.

A strike which was controlled by the rank-and-file could have put such tactics into practice, and stepped up picketing (including in front of the Grammy awards). It also could have raised key demands to unionize all "reality show" and animation writers and match the new contract's expiration date to that of the Screen Actors Guild (SAG) and DAG, thus allowing for the possibility of future strikes to shut down all production on both coasts.

The Screen Actors Guild's contract with the AMPTP is set to expire in July. The members of SAG, many of whom have been very supportive of the striking writers, may strike then, breaking with the past tradition of "pattern bargaining" (making agreements with the AMPTP similar to those recently made by the WGA and DGA).

A strategy for victory at Stella D'Oro

Sisters and brothers:

You have been on strike for months with little progress to speak of. As we are drawing up this statement, scabs are inside of the factory, doing your jobs. While your struggle is doubtless one that needs to be waged, and an inspiration to workers everywhere, it's clear that changes in strategy must be made if you are to move forward.

It is for that reason that we are reaching out to you. We hope the following will help you in the battle against your bosses.

The problem with unions

The unions in this country were born out of militant struggles by the working class. But over the years, the militancy that gave birth to the unions has been beaten out of them. A combination of government interference, anti-communist witch hunts and union busting have left the unions weak and under the control of privileged bureaucrats who have more in common with your bosses than you. This shows!

The bureaucrats at the top of the unions bind workers to the bosses and their representatives in government. They push the myth that you have interests in common with those who exploit you. The fact is you and your bosses share no common interests. The bosses want to get as much labor out of you as they can for as little money as possible. You want to get what you deserve for your labor, as you should.

In *this* struggle, your hands are being tied by the very bureaucrats that claim to represent you. You are corralled off to the side of the plant gate, under the watchful eye of the NYPD (whose presence makes scabbing possible), all with the union leadership's approval. Your struggle is kept quiet. While the

AFL-CIO was happy to give $1,138,368 away to rich politicians in the last election, it can't come up with enough money to publicize your strike or keep you and your families financially stable today. Even in the December 2008 edition of your union's newsletter "BCTGM Report," your strike only received two sentences of coverage. Several supporters who came to your last rally said they had no idea you were even on strike!

It is *you*, the workers who are on strike, who must wage it, independently of those who are limiting your ability.

A city-wide boycott

Nearly every grocery store in this city is unionized. A boycott of all Stella D'oro products should be launched for the duration of your strike. You should make a list of grocery stores in the city then divide them up amongst yourselves. Each worker can visit several stores directly, to appeal to the workers there to refuse to handle any Stella D'oro products. In return, you can promise to back any struggles of theirs which may come up in the future.

You should also reach out to any and all workers who bring materials into the plant or take finished products away. Do whatever you need to do to convince them not to carry anything to or from the plant.

Leafleting and informational picketing should also be done outside the biggest grocery stores, as well as those in working class neighborhoods. This can boost the visibility and effectiveness of a boycott, and pressure the stores into dropping Stella D'oro products.

Reach out

You should elect groups from amongst yourselves to go to the meetings of every other union in the city and appeal to the rank-and-file for support.

Plan a real mass rally. Reach out to every union and pro-labor organization in the tri-state area for support. Show the bosses where your fellow workers stand.

Your strike and the boycott should be widely publicized. Fight to get your union to shell out the necessary funds to place high profile ads in publications, on radio and on TV. Demand it! Your dues are what makes the union go!

Shouts don't stop production

Every day you are forced to witness scabs crossing your picket line and entering the plant. They are doing your jobs and keeping the plant running. The bosses and their government have laws and enforcers in place that keep you off to the side, unable to prevent the scabs from entering and exiting. Your only recourse is to shout at them as you watch them come and go. But your shouts don't stop them.

Your power as workers lies in your position in the process of production. A strike is powerful because by withdrawing your labor you bring production to a halt. The bosses can't make a profit when their plants are shut down. But when scabs freely cross your picket line, the power of your strike is seriously undercut. Scabbing must be prevented if you are to win.

Your livelihood is at stake. You must do what you have to do to win!

You should reach out to all workers in the city, union and non-union alike, and call for mass picketing in front of the plant. Workers are fed up with being kicked around and many are awakening. Well publicized calls for mass picketing have the possibility of bringing a large number of your fellow workers to your aid.

Take care of yourselves

You must keep your collective well being in mind. Don't let any of your members fall into dire straits.

Work together as a group to solve individual problems.

We stand in solidarity

We stand in unfaltering solidarity with you in your struggle. We are more than willing to mobilize our members, supporters and allies for your cause. We propose that a public meeting be held to discuss your struggle. Such a meeting, held under a title such as "Workers Are Fighting Back," could draw in a number of workers from around the city. The meeting could consist of discussions about your strike as well as the recent worker occupation of the Republic Windows factory in Chicago and the current wave of strikes in Italy. You all could elect one or two workers from your own ranks to give a talk about your fight, and a hat could be passed around to collect donations to help you make it through this difficult time. We would cover all expenses and hand any donations that come of the event directly to you, the rank-and-file workers.

We are also more than willing to help you publicize any boycott efforts or carry out other required work. As well, our means of communication are open to you. We welcome your comments, letters, articles, etc., and we would be glad to interview any of you either in print or on video to help publicize and build support for your struggle.

If you are interested in our assistance or want to discuss any of this, please do not hesitate to contact us.

GM offers buyouts to auto workers in bid to eliminate union jobs

On Tuesday, February 19, 2008, General Motors offered buyouts to everyone of its 74,000 hourly employees in a renewed attempt to rip apart their union, the United Auto Workers (UAW). By offering the buyouts, GM seeks to get rid of every union worker and flout contract obligations by hiring low-paid, non-union replacements. In order to increase their profits exponentially, GM is offering higher amounts to those workers who agree to give up their retirement and healthcare plans.

GM previously offered buyouts to workers in 2006, helping it to eliminate some 40,000 union jobs.

Ford offered similar buyouts to all 54,000 hourly workers at its plants in January.

The elimination of better paying union jobs and benefits that were won in bitter battles is what has come out of the "partnership" between the auto bosses and the workers of the UAW that has been consistently pushed by union bureaucrats. These union tops, separated from the workers they supposedly represent by their position and privilege, serve to hold back the activities of the rank-and-file while lining their own pockets.

The truth is that workers and bosses have diametrically opposed interests. All "partnerships" between the two equate to curtailing workers' struggles – in the name of "working together" – long enough to give the bosses time regroup and conjure up plans for an inevitable frontal assault.

What's needed is cooperation among the workers themselves, to get around obstacles put in their way by union tops and fight to pursue their own interests.

Workers at GM and Ford should reach out to the 2,500

165

members of UAW Local 2069 who are currently striking the Volvo truck plant in Dublin, Virginia and others in the union to organize such a struggle.

An overview of the world financial crisis

Unless you've been living on a deserted island for the past few months you know of the world financial crisis that is unfolding.

A number of the world's biggest banks have crashed, surviving only through massive financial injections from world governments. The stock markets in Asia, Europe and the Americas have lost over $25 trillion dollars since the beginning of 2008. Over one million people in the U.S. alone have lost their jobs in the same period. South Korea's stock market index has fallen 42.6 percent. Countries from Singapore to the U.S. to Germany are "officially" in recession. News continues to come in at a rate that makes it impossible for us to keep up with, but needless to say things are only continuing to get worse.

And it's not nearly over. Jacques Attali, economic adviser to French president Nicolas Sarkozy, warns of "A tsunami on the way." The International Monetary Fund has said 50 countries will be hit by famine. The International Labour Organization predicts that at least 20 million jobs will be lost by the end of 2009, bringing the total number of unemployed people in the world to 200 million, the highest in recorded history. They're joined by a slue of other economists, spokesmen, and government officials who also warn of things to come.

So, what caused this world financial crisis?

According to many world leaders, business leaders, bankers, and their mouthpieces in the corporate-owned media, the current crisis is a result of "excesses" or "bad management."

The truth is that recessions are endemic to capitalism, the form of society in which we live. In the last forty-one years alone there have been five recessions (1967, 1974, 1981, 1991,

2001). Before that, there were many, many more, including the Great Depression.

Roughly every ten years, capitalism goes through a cyclical crisis or "business cycle" of "boom and bust."

While capitalism is in a "boom phase," or period of expansion, products are regularly bought up because a lot people have money. But because a lot of people have it, the value of money goes down, causing prices to simultaneously rise. This is called inflation.

In the boom phase, labor is needed to meet the increased demands for goods and services. As workers rush to fill the newly opened positions, unemployment falls.

Businesses see profit being made and want to increase their involvement, causing them to seek funding through credit. The bankers want to get in on the action too, so they raise the interest rates on loans they give out.

The rise in interest rates slows down the demand for credit. The debts of those who borrowed to take part in the expansion begin to build up. Production starts to slow down. Unemployment rises. As a combination of job losses and inflation, people can no longer afford to buy things as they did before. The boom phase draws to a close and the crisis begins.

As production and incomes decline, the bankers get nervous and call in their loans, but because of declining sales the business owners cannot afford to pay them. This leads to bankruptcies and loan defaults. Businesses cannot afford to take out new loans at the current interest rates, so the bankers are forced to lower their interest rates. Increased unemployment and desperation among working people leads them to take lower paying jobs.

After a while, lower prices lead overstocked shelves to begin to empty and bad debts are written off. Businesses see the low wages and prices that have come about as new profit-making opportunities, and the whole cycle starts over again.

Of course the scope and impact of each crisis depends on the scope of the credit system. The more credit is extended, the bigger the crisis.

The current crisis is so serious for precisely this reason.

In the 1970's, another crisis occurred. In the richer countries like the U.S., businesses saw the slow rise of workers' wages (which themselves came about as a result of struggles, unionization, etc.) as an obstacle to profit making, so they began moving their operations to poor countries in which workers earned substantially lower wages (also known as "outsourcing"), bringing in workers from poor countries to work for lower wages, and replacing manned-positions with computers and/or machines. In one respect, this was a huge success. The businesses were able to produce the same products and services as they had before at a much lower cost, leading to a vast increase in their profits. On the other hand though, their maneuvers caused the workers' wages to either stagnate or fall, which meant that they could no longer buy products as fast as they were being made.

In order to keep their profits increasing the businesses extended credit to the workers. This was the only way to keep selling their increasing number of products while real wages continued to stand still or fall. But it wasn't a permanent fix. It simply postponed the crisis.

Throughout the 1980's, 1990's and the first few years of the 2000's, consumer lending (credit to workers) exploded. While allowing millions to continue to buy products and services, it also drove millions into crushing debt. By 2006, those U.S. workers in the worst financial conditions (the "sub-prime" borrowers), couldn't keep up. This was the first crack in the hollow shell. Capitalism being an interconnected world system, the crack could only spread. Today the shell is shattering completely.

As a result of the Great Depression in the 1930's (the biggest crisis of capitalism to date), governments came to see the need to interfere with capitalism (that is to adjust interest rates, exchange rates, etc.) in an attempt to prevent future crises. But the more credit, speculation (the buying and selling of stocks, real estate, bonds, etc., to profit from fluctuations in prices) and money with no real basis (money which is just paper and doesn't represent anything real of value) build up and comes to dominate the world economy (which is happening more and more each day), the more difficult it is to stave off crisis. The current crisis has proved that.

So, who was Marx, and what does he have to do with all of this?

Karl Marx was a political economist and political theorist, but above all, he was a revolutionary. Among his many writings was Capital, an exposé of the workings of the exploitative capitalist system. But Marx didn't just criticize capitalism, he also pointed the way forward for humanity, through the creation of a higher form of social organization. Marx lived from 1818 to 1883, but his theories remain as relevant today as when they were first written.

What Marx Said

"The ultimate reason for all real crises always remains the poverty and restricted consumption of the masses as opposed to the drive of capitalist production to develop the productive forces as though only the absolute consuming power of society constituted their limit." - *Capital, Volume III*, Chapter 30.

"...[I]n the same measure in which the capitalists are compelled.... to exploit the already existing gigantic means of production on an ever-increasing scale, and for this purpose to set in motion all the mainsprings of credit, in the same measure do they increase the industrial earthquakes, in the midst of which the commercial world can preserve itself only by sacrificing a portion of its wealth, its products, and even its forces of production, to the gods of the lower world – in short, the crises increase. They become more frequent and more violent, if for no other reason, than for this alone, that in the same measure in which the mass of products grows, and there the needs for extensive markets, in the same measure does the world market shrink ever more, and ever fewer markets remain to be exploited, since every previous crisis has subjected to the commerce of the world a hitherto unconquered or but superficially exploited market." - *Wage-Labor & Capital*, Chapter 9.

"Contradiction in the capitalist mode of production: the laborers as buyers of commodities are important for the market. But as sellers of their own commodity — labor-power — capitalist society tends to keep them down to the minimum price.

"Further contradiction: the periods in which capitalist production exerts all its forces regularly turn out to be periods of over-production, because production potentials can never be utilised to such an extent that more value may not only be produced but also realised; but the sale of commodities, the realisation of commodity-capital and thus of surplus-value, is limited, not by the consumer requirements of society in general, but by the consumer requirements of a society in which the vast majority are always poor and must always remain poor." - *Capital*, Volume II, Chapter 16.

"The enormous power, inherent in the factory system, of expanding by jumps, and the dependence of that system on the markets of the world, necessarily beget feverish production, followed by over-filling of the markets, whereupon contraction of the markets brings on crippling of production. The life of modern industry becomes a series of periods of moderate activity, prosperity, over-production, crisis and stagnation. The uncertainty and instability to which machinery subjects the employment, and consequently the conditions of existence, of the operatives become normal, owing to these periodic changes of the industrial cycle. Except in the periods of prosperity, there rages between the capitalists the most furious combat for the share of each in the markets. This share is directly proportional to the cheapness of the. product. Besides the rivalry that this struggle begets in the application of improved machinery for replacing labor-power, and of new methods of production, there also comes a time in every industrial cycle, when a forcible reduction of wages beneath the value of labor-power, is attempted for the purpose of cheapening commodities.

"A necessary condition, therefore, to the growth of the number of factory hands, is a proportionally much more rapid growth of the amount of capital invested in mills. This growth, however, is conditioned by the ebb and flow of the industrial cycle. It is, besides, constantly interrupted by the technical progress that at one time virtually supplies the place of new workmen, at another, actually displaces old ones. This qualitative change in mechanical industry continually discharges hands from the factory, or shuts its doors against the fresh stream of recruits, while the purely quantitative extension of the factories absorbs not only the men thrown out of work, but also fresh contingents. The workpeople are thus continually both repelled and attracted, hustled from pillar to post, while, at the same time, constant changes take place in the sex, age, and skill of the levies." - *Capital*, Volume I, Chapter 25.

"In every stockjobbing swindle every one knows that some time or other the crash must come, but every one hopes that it may fall on the head of his neighbour, after he himself has caught the shower of gold and placed it in safety. Après moi le déluge! is the watchword of every capitalist and of every capitalist nation. Hence Capital is reckless of the health or length of life of the laborer, unless under compulsion from society." - *Capital*, Volume I, Chapter 10.

"After every crisis there are enough ex-manufacturers in the English factory districts who will supervise, for low wages, what were formerly their own factories in the capacity of managers of the new owners, who are frequently their creditors." - *Capital*, Volume III, Chapter 23.

"In the social production of their existence, men inevitably enter into definite relations, which are independent of their will, namely relations of production appropriate to a given stage in the development of their material forces of production. The totality of these relations of production constitutes the economic structure of society, the real foundation, on which arises a legal and political superstructure and to which correspond definite forms of social consciousness. The mode of production of material life conditions the general process of social, political and intellectual life. It is not the consciousness of men that determines their existence, but their social existence that determines their consciousness. At a certain stage of development, the material productive forces of society come into conflict with the existing relations of production or — this merely expresses the same thing in legal terms — with the property relations within the framework of which they have operated hitherto. From forms of development of the productive forces these relations turn into their fetters. Then begins an era of social revolution. The changes in the economic foundation lead sooner or later to the transformation of the whole immense superstructure." - *Preface to the Contribution to the Critique of Political Economy*

The solution

At one time in history capitalism was progressive. That time is long gone.

Today, capitalism is a fetter on human development. It is a system based on the exploitation of the working majority for the benefit of a parasitic minority. It has outlived its historical usefulness and has entered a period of decline, with dire consequences for humanity.

The for-profit system is at the end of its rope. It offers

no way out for the suffering masses. Instead it contributes to their suffering! Today, as millions—even in the richest countries —are being forced into homelessness and unemployment, while tens of thousands around the world continue to die every day as a result of starvation and curable disease, human labor and valuable resources are squandered on useless gimmicks and weapons that can destroy the human species and the earth itself. The world provides enough for every human being to have a quality life, yet capitalism restricts those without enough money from even surviving.

It is necessary for humanity to sweep away capitalism and replace it with a higher form of social organization. Because of its position in capitalist society as the producers of all, the sole force capable of carrying out this task is the working class (made up of all those who have no way to survive other than by selling themselves piecemeal, e.g. by the hour for a wage, to a capitalist who profits from their work).

The working class must oust the capitalist parasites and take power and control of production into their own hands, in order to reorganize society to meet human need. Only the rule of the working class can reverse humanity's slide in barbarism, create a society free of exploitation and oppression, and pave the way for the creation of a world of material abundance in which the needs of all are met.

Marx correctly described the evolution of human society and the workings of the capitalist system as we have shown here. But as Marx said long ago, the point is not simply to understand the world, but to change it!

Obama and McCain: Two sides of the same imperialist coin

As the 2008 presidential elections approach, a growing crisis is engulfing the United States and the rest of the world. Not knowing where to look for answers, millions of people inside and out of the U.S. are placing their hopes in the outcome of this contest.

The mainstream media and supporters of both candidates are going all out to convince us of the importance of this "decisive election," but as we will show, Barrack Obama and John McCain are simply two "new" versions of the same old crap.

The sham of "democracy" in the United States

Democracy means government of the people, but it is not the people that rule in the U.S.

The majority of the U.S. population has opposed the war in Iraq for years, yet the U.S. government continues to wage it unabated.

Millions turned out to vote for candidates from the Democratic Party in the 2006 midterm elections in hopes that they would work to end the war in Iraq only to have those same politicians continue to authorize it once in office.

If there were truly a "government of the people" in the United States, the war in Iraq would have ended long ago and public funds would be used on things like education and healthcare instead of bombs and corporate handouts.

Two parties, one master

In our society the population is, for the most part, divided into two camps: the toiling masses that have to work to survive and the rich capitalist minority that profits from their work. It is that capitalist elite which rules–by virtue of its control of all the factories, transportation and distribution networks, etc.—and the politics of the country reflect that.

Every president since 1853 has belonged to either the Democratic or Republican Party.

Both the Democrats and the Republicans represent the same ruling capitalist elite. Both parties receive their major funding from the same corporations and banks. Wal-Mart gives nearly the same amount of money to the Democratic Party as it does the Republican Party. Pfizer and AT&T do the same. Other corporations, like Home Depot and AFLAC, give a little more to the Democrats, but still make sure to donate substantially to the Republicans.

The list goes on and on.

As the saying goes, he who pays the piper calls the tune.

Because both Obama and McCain represent the same group of people, their policies are fundamentally the same. Any differences between them are primarily strategic. In other words, they differ only in what they think is the best way for the capitalists to rule.

Minor differences, major similarities

Even on issues of strategy, Obama and McCain have very few differences.

In early October, both Senators voted in for the widely unpopular Wall Street "bailout," doing their parts in the government's move to hand over *at least* $700 billion in federal funds to Treasury Secretary Henry Paulson, which he will distribute to the very banks and financial institutions that helped create the very financial crisis the "bailout" is supposed to help

176

resolve. Obama and McCain's votes also helped secure $150 billion in tax cuts to businesses and the wealthy. When asked who they would choose to serve as Treasury Secretary were they to become president, both candidates have suggested billionaire investor Warren Buffet, an iconic member of the capitalist class they serve.

Both candidates support anti-democratic legislation such as the USA PATRIOT Act and government spying on U.S. citizens.

On the issue of war, the candidates have some differences—though not of the kind you may imagine.

For the last several years, a key criticism of George W. Bush by many Democrats has been that he tied down troops in Iraq that could have been better used elsewhere. The Democrats aren't against war, they just think that Bush decided to wage it in the wrong place.

Obama subscribes to this outlook wholeheartedly. While posing as an "anti-war" candidate in order to "rein in" the tens of millions of people in the United States who oppose the war in Iraq, Obama actually plans to expand the massive U.S. war machine.

Colin Kahl, Obama's top adviser on Iraq, recently penned a report for the imperialist think tank Center for a New American Security in which he stated that in Iraq, "the U.S. should aim to transition to a sustainable over-watch posture (of perhaps 60,000-80,000 forces) by the end of 2010."

Richard Danzig, Obama's chief national security adviser, recently told the press that if elected, Obama would massively increase U.S. military spending (which is already equal to the military budgets of all the other countries in the world *combined*) before saying that Bush's Pentagon chief, Robert Gates, would make an "even better [chief] in an Obama administration."

Obama chose Zbigniew Brzezinski, the former National

Security Advisor under President Jimmy Carter who engineered the "Carter Doctrine" which stated that the U.S. would use force to secure oil in the Persian Gulf, to be his foreign policy adviser.

Obama's running mate, Senator Joseph Biden, elaborated on he and Obama's militarist ambitions during the October 2, 2008, vice-presidential debates, promising to step up the war in Afghanistan, launch new military excursions into Pakistan, take a harder line towards the Venezuelan and Bolivian governments (which have committed the unforgivable crime of attempting to move away from U.S. domination), and increase the U.S. government's support to the criminal Israeli regime in its continued efforts to squash Palestinian and Lebanese resistance.

This militarism differs from McCain's only in which countries will fall into the cross-hairs. McCain, dubbed a "war hero" by his opponent and the capitalist press for being taken prison by Vietnamese forces after being shot down while flying over that country with the intention of dropping bombs on it for the 23rd time, will focus the U.S. war machine more on Iran, Sudan and Myanmar.

Of course on the question of war the candidates also have a lot in common—both with each other and with current president George W. Bush.

The Wall Street Journal, a mouthpiece of the capitalist class in the United States, recently admitted as much in an op-ed entitled "Don't Expect a Big Change in U.S. Foreign Policy," which candidly stated "Regardless of who wins in November, the current foreign policy will live on in the next White House."

Both Obama and McCain seek to strengthen the ranks of the U.S. volunteer army for new military missions abroad. Both have publicly criticized college universities that no longer allow the military's Reserved Officer Training Corps (ROTC) on their campuses. (The ROTC was driven off of many campuses as a result of popular protests against them during the U.S. invasion of Viet Nam.) Both call on young people in the United States to have a "willingness to sacrifice," that is, to put their lives on the line for the financial gain of their rich capitalist rulers.

Obama the socialist?

In spite of the ridiculous claims of some of the more extreme right-wing talking heads that Obama is some sort of "socialist" who wants to take from the rich and give to the poor, he is fully dedicated to the capitalist system. As *Left Business Observer* put it in March, 2008, "big capital would have no problem with an Obama presidency... [Top hedge fund managers] think he's the man to do their work," and "They're confident he wouldn't undertake any renovations to the distribution of wealth."

The Democrats are not "pro-worker"

In the limited "labor movement" that currently exists in the U.S., the Democrats are often viewed as more friendly to workers than the Republicans. In our country, which unlike most other countries in the world doesn't even have a party *pretending* to represent the working class, many thus view the Democrats as "pro-worker."

That the Democrats sometimes mouth pro-worker rhetoric during election season doesn't change their class character one bit. When push comes to shove that fact becomes obvious.

When transit workers in New York City went out on strike in 2005, Democrat Eliot Spitzer, then-New York State Attorney General, hit their union with legal injunctions and millions of dollars in fines. New York Senator Hillary Clinton, herself a leading Democrat, supported Spitzer's earlier use of the anti-worker Taylor Law against those same workers in 1999.

In 1985, Rudy Perpich, the Democratic governor of

Minnesota, called out the National Guard to break the picket line of striking workers at the Hormel meatpacking plant in Austin and usher scab "replacement workers" into the workplace.

These are just two examples of many.

Over the last several decades, union membership has declined as decent jobs have been increasingly replaced by part-time "McJobs." This has brought along with it a colossal drop in pay and benefits. In 2006, *The New York Times* reported that "wages and salaries now make up the lowest share of the nation's gross domestic product since the government began recording the data in 1947, while corporate profits have climbed to their highest share since the 1960's."

The Democrats joined the Republicans in working on behalf of the capitalists they represent by overseeing and helping along the processes that have lead to these conditions.

Still, the bureaucrats who lead what's left of the unions in the U.S. today continue to tie the working people they supposedly represent to the capitalist Democratic Party!

The utter treachery of such misleaders is aptly demonstrated by the current situation of the International Association of Machinists (IAM). While the 27,000 members of that union who have been out on strike against the Boeing Corporation for over a month are forced to eek out a living on the meager $150 strike pay they receive from the union each week, their union's leaders are funneling millions of dollars into the record-setting campaign fund of multimillionaire Barrack Obama.

The Democrats are not and cannot be an "anti-war" party

Many people in the U.S. falsely see the Democrats as an "anti-war" party. History tells a different story. Democratic presidents were in office during the invasion of Haiti in 1915, the invasions of the Dominican Republic in both 1916 and 1965, the invasion of Russia in 1918, the invasion of Korea in 1950, the invasion of Viet Nam in 1963, the "humanitarian" bombings of Yugoslavia throughout the 1990's, the bombings of Afghanistan and Sudan in 1998, and the mercenary invasion of Cuba in 1961, among others. Former president Bill Clinton, a favorite of the party, sent more troops to more parts of the world than any U.S. president since World War II.

The fact is that the United States is an imperialist country. The capitalist ruling class has to constantly look for ways to increase its profits, both in the U.S. and internationally. This leads it to carry out political and military actions of all sorts, from discreet palace coups to outright invasions, in order to secure new resources, markets and cheap labor and generally create conditions more favorable to its domination of the world. A change in presidents cannot change this fundamental fact. Nothing short of the elimination of imperialism can bring an end to war once and for all.

An historical election?

Much is being made of the "ground breaking" prospects of having either the first Black president or the first female vice-president. This kind of identity politics is the norm in the circus that is electoral politics in the United States.

Innocent Iraqis are no more pleased to be shot by an Arab-American member of the U.S. Army than a white one.

The fact that two of the three cops that shot 44 bullets into Sean Bell (an innocent, unarmed Black man murdered by members of the NYPD) in 2006 were minorities is certainly of no comfort to his family.

STOP ERA, one of the most prominent anti-feminist organizations in the U.S., was founded by Phyllis Schlafy, a woman.

181

While a person's ideas are shaped by their surroundings, their politics and/or actions are not dictated by their nationality or sex. To claim otherwise is itself a form of discrimination that arbitrarily and incorrectly attaches certain views to certain people.

A lesser evil?

The condition of "democracy" in the U.S. is so poor that many who vote do so solely in an attempt to keep the candidate they think is worse out of office. In other words, they don't vote for a candidate because they support his or her politics, but simply because they view him or her as "less bad" than the other candidate.

Even if one candidate *really was* much worse than the other, this kind of strategy would be the equivalent of requesting to be shot by a rifle instead of a canon.

In politics, one is defined much more by what they are actually for than what they are against.

Get out the vote

Many people in the U.S. are already keenly aware of the fallacious nature of elections in this country which is why a large percentage of the eligible portion of the population doesn't even both to vote.

This year, the capitalists hope to change that trend.

With plans to greatly expand and enforce their domination, the capitalist rulers are seeking to win regular people over to their rehashed program of imperialism through a combination of jingoistic rhetoric and propaganda from the corporate media.

They are counting on a high voter turnout to give an air of legitimacy to their "democratic" system as they continue their global plunder, drawing mass opposition from millions of people both at home and abroad.

By putting forth Obama as an agent of "change" and McCain as an agent of "reform," they seek to pull millions of discontent and outright angry people back into the "acceptable realm" of electoral politics. By doing so, they hope to lessen the possibility of future protests, strikes and other expressions of dissatisfaction which could in anyway challenge their rule.

In the end, whether or not you cast a vote in November will have no real bearing on the future. Our intentions are to shatter illusions in the twin parties of the capitalist elite and present a viable alternative.

Obamamania: Dreams of change and the hard reality

On Tuesday, November 4, 2008, Democratic Party candidate Barrack Obama, the self-anointed "candidate of change," was elected President of the United States of American in a landslide victory.

Obama is the first Black person to be elected President of the United States.

Of course, he didn't run as a Black man but as an American who pushed the myth of "National Unity."

Still, liberals and reformists – and even some who claim to be revolutionaries – have pointed to Obama's election as some sort of historic victory for Black people. This amounts to dead-end identity politics and nothing more.

What does the election of a Black man mean to the 900,000 Black men and women currently in the U.S. prison system? What does it mean for the 48 percent of Black men between the ages of 18 and 65 in New York City who are unemployed? What does it mean for the 40 percent of Black children across the country who live in poverty? What does it mean for Addie Polk, the 90-year-old Black woman in Akron, Ohio, who attempted suicide by shooting herself in the chest twice out of desperation over a bank foreclosure on her home? What does it mean for Dantaze Story, an unarmed 29-year Black man shot dead by Los Angeles police on November 11, 2008, and his family? What does it mean for Black people in the United States? Absolutely nothing!

Those who falsely believe that personal characteristics such as race, sex, etc., of the leaders of their country has anything to do with their politics or what they will do once in office would be wise to review history.

In South Africa, the racist white-minority apartheid government was dismantled in 1994 and Nelson Mandela, leader of the African National Congress (ANC), which fought against apartheid for decades, was elected president. While this was hailed as a great victory at the time, the lives of the Black majority didn't improve. Now, after 14 years of ANC rule, conditions for most remain the same, or have worsened!

One could also look at India and Pakistan, where the hideous oppression of women not only continued but reached terrifying new heights while those countries had female heads of state. There are many more examples.

Obama's supporters point to his election as "proof" that racism is dead, or at least dying. They neglect to mention that Obama actually lost the "white vote" by twelve percentage points. They also forget, or at least forget to mention, that the rise of Obama's campaign brought with it an increase in racist attacks and provocations – to go along with the racist assaults which are a regular part of life in the U.S..

On the night of Obama's election, Ali Kamara, a Black teenager in New York City, was beaten by a crowd of white men with baseball bats chanting "Obama." Days later, on November 8, a group of white teenagers who set out to "hunt a Mexican" brutally murdered Marcelo Lucero, an Ecuadorian immigrant who had been living and working in the U.S. for 18 years, in Long Island.

The "racism is dead" and "we're all united as Americans" crap pushed by Obama and parroted by the liberals and reformists is already being used by right wingers to attack the very people are who supposedly no longer oppressed.

William Bennett, the former Secretary of Education who infamously stated, "[I]f you wanted to reduce crime, you could ... abort every black baby in this country, and your crime rate would go down," is now pointing to the election of Obama as a reason not to "take any excuses anymore from anybody [read: Black person] who says, 'The deck is stacked, I can't do anything, there's so much in-built this and that.'" As if a legacy of over 400 years of oppression can be eliminated with the election of a Black man to the position of president!

And what about the change Obama promises? The only change we see is a change in Obama's promises themselves.

As is often the case in Democratic Party primaries, Obama begin his campaign by posing as someone to the "left" of the existing political establishment. He did this both to win over the party's liberal base and to bring the millions of people who had become disgusted with "politics" as they exist in the United States, or who never gave a damn to begin with, back into the fold. It's no coincidence that the "candidate of change" was put forward in the same period as popular support of both the Republicans and Democrats dropped to historic lows.

By promoting the lie that "change" could be brought about through elections, Obama was able to build a renewed enthusiasm in "democracy" and integrate people who were otherwise hostile to the rulers and their system into it.

Obama originally promised to sign the Employee Free Choice Act, which would enable workers to gain union recognition by card check instead of having to wait for an election, into law. Soon after his election however, the *Wall Street Journal* – mouthpiece of the capitalist elite – warned that the bill, along with "efforts to regulate greenhouse gas emissions, and a slew of contemplated taxes" would likely take a "back seat" while Obama focused his energy on handing public funds over to floundering corporations.

In the beginning of his campaign, Obama posed as an "anti-war" candidate. As time went on however, it became clear that did not actually oppose war to begin with. Obama selected Zbigniew Brzezinski, the architect of the "Carter Doctrine" of using force to secure oil in the Persian Gulf, as foreign policy adviser during his campaign. He raised calls to shift troops from

Iraq to Afghanistan, where a supposedly "good war" is being waged at the cost of the lives of countless innocent civilians. He selected Joe Biden – who calls for more troops in Afghanistan, more military incursions into Pakistan and increased pressure on Venezuela and Bolivia – as his running mate. If anything, Obama, like other leading Democrats, simply thought that the U.S. had tied down troops in Iraq which could have been used better to secure capitalist interests elsewhere. Even still, as the elections grew closer Obama's advisers cautioned that while he would like to withdraw troops from Iraq "as soon as possible" it would be a question he "will revisit when he becomes president." As it stands, it appears that Obama plans a "phased withdraw" that will see U.S. troops in Iraq long into 2010, or possibly longer.

Any claim that a candidate put forward by the Democratic Party is or could be "anti-war" is ludicrous. A cursory examination of U.S. history shows that Democrats were in the White House during the U.S. invasions and/or bombings of Viet Nam, Korea, Cuba, Haiti, Sudan, Yugoslavia, Afghanistan (1998), Russia and the Dominican Republic (twice).

Indeed, Obama's "transition team" is *already* looking into options for a preemptive attack on Iran. Obama has chosen Hilary Clinton, who during the primaries threatened to "totally obliterate" Iran, and who he previously attacked for supporting the war in Iraq, as Secretary of State.

Obama's other picks come directly from the political establishment he claims to differ from. Thirty-one of the 47 people chosen so far also served under President Bill Clinton. One of the more notable picks is Rahm Emanuel, a former chief adviser of Bill Clinton who championed the former president's gutting of welfare and vocally supported the invasion of Iraq, as Chief of Staff. Another notable appointment is that of Lawrence Summers, who wrote "the economic logic behind dumping a load of toxic waste in the lowest wage country is impeccable" in

187

a leaked World Bank memo in 1991, as director of the National Economic Council. Finally, we must mention Obama's reporter pick of Eric Holder, a "law-and-order" attorney appointed to several judicial and prosecutorial positions by both Democrats and Republicans whose most famous case involved his defense of Chiquita Brands International Inc. against charges of aiding terrorism for its admitted support to right-wing death squads in Colombia, as Attorney General.

Reports also indicate that Obama will keep FBI Director Robert Mueller, who oversaw the U.S. government's program of spying on tens of thousands of people's phone calls, emails, financial records and other information, in his position. John Brennan, the top CIA aid to George Tenet under George W. Bush who vocally supports torture and calls government sponsored kidnapping "a vital tool," is Obama's chief for intelligence policy. There have also been media reports that Obama will ask Robert Gates, architect of the bloody "surge" in Iraq, to remain as Secretary of Defense. So much for change!

Yet liberals and reformists alike *still* continue to promote illusions in Obama. We're told that we're witnessing the "dawn of a new era!"

The fact is Obama is a capitalist politician who belongs to one of the twin parties of capitalist dictatorship. He represents the interests of the same ruling elite as McCain would have, only in a different way. *That's why* both campaigns received massive amounts of funding from corporations like Wal-Mart and Pfizer. *That's why* both candidates supported the $700 billion corporate bailout. *That's why* both candidates supported the same person for Secretary of the Treasury. *That's why* both candidates support the US-PATRIOT act and domestic spying. *That's why* both candidates pledged to build up the already-overinflated U.S. military machine. *That's why* the *Wall Street Journal* wrote that "Regardless of who wins in November, the current foreign policy will live on in the next White House." *That's why* regardless of who won the elections,

188

workers lost. *That's why* we opposed Obama and McCain equally.

Of course in this period of "Obamamania" our position is not a very popular one. But we are proletarian revolutionaries, we stand on principle and we constantly bring the interests of the working class to the front. We're not seeking to win fleeting popularity. Whether or not a position is correct is not determined by how many people hold it at a given time. From now through at least the early months of Obama's presidency we will have to go "against the grain," but that's fine. Going against the grain is far from alien to revolutionaries.

The reason we expose the poison being put forward by the liberals and the reformist is to contrast it with the only true way forward for humanity: proletarian revolution, in which the rule of the warmongering capitalist elite is smashed and replaced with the rule of the working majority.

Only such a thoroughgoing revolution, which expropriates the expropriators and rips ups the very roots of oppression, can end the exploitation of the working majority and financial crises once and for all, reorganize the economy to meet human need and begin to answer for the historical crimes committed against Blacks and other oppressed nations (such as the Native Americans).

As Vladamir Lenin pointed out in his famous text *The State and Revolution*, "In capitalist society, providing it develops under the most favorable conditions, we have a more or less complete democracy in the democratic republic. But this democracy is always hemmed in by the narrow limits set by capitalist exploitation, and consequently always remains, in effect, a democracy for the minority, only for the propertied classes, only for the rich. Freedom in capitalist society always remains about the same as it was in the ancient Greek republics: freedom for the slave-owners.... Democracy for an insignificant minority, democracy for the rich - that is the democracy of capitalist society."

Political Prisoners in the United States

While Washington continually condemns the governments of countries it opposes for violations of human rights, the crimes of the rulers of "friendly countries" like Saudi Arabia are ignored. Even more to the point, activities by the U.S. government itself that mirror the regimes of other "evil countries" go largely unmentioned.

Collected here are profiles on some of the most high-profile political prisoners in the United States today.

Mumia Abu Jamal

Mumia Abu-Jamal is an award-winning journalist who has been on death row since 1982, falsely accused of the murder of Philadelphia police officer Daniel Faulkner.

The State of Pennsylvania claims that in 1981, Mumia, then a cab driver, saw his brother being beaten by Officer Faulkner across the street from where he was parked. They claim he ran over and shot Faulkner in the back, was in turn shot by Faulkner, and then shot Faulkner several more times in the head. The facts do not bare these claims out.

At trial, the prosecution's main eyewitness was a prostitute named Cynthia White. White claimed she say Mumia run across a parking lot with a gun, but two other prostitutes and another woman who knew her have since stated that White was coerced by police into giving this testimony. Two other eyewitnesses say that White wasn't even on the corner in question when the shooting occurred.

Pamela Jenkins, another prostitute, says other police officers were present at Faulkner's shooting and that Cynthia White was an informant who regularly preformed sexual favors to cops.

The prosecution's other "eyewitness," a cab driver named Robert Chobert, now admits to receiving favors in exchange for his testimony. He also stated that he wasn't even in a location that would allow him to witness the shooting, a fact backed up by newly discovered photos of the crime scene.

Another key piece of "evidence" provided by the prosecution is a supposed confession made by Mumia as he lay on a hospital bed recovering from his gunshot wound. But no police officer claimed to hear a confession by Mumia until two months after it supposedly took place. In fact, a police officer who watched over Mumia the night of the shooting stated that he "made no comments." The police "suddenly" recalled his confession immediately after he filed charges of police brutality.

Vietnam War veteran and small business owner William Singletary, who was at the scene of the shooting, reported to police that the shooter was wearing a green army jacket and that Mumia didn't arrive on the scene until after Faulkner had been shot. For this he was repeatedly threatened, his gas station was vandalized, and he was eventually run out of town altogether.

Others, including two police officers, also said the shooter was wearing a green army jacket. Mumia was wearing a red quilted jacket the night of the shooting. Other witnesses also say they saw someone running from the scene. Mumia was found shot at the scene.

Dessie Hightower, one of the witnesses who saw someone running from the scene of the shooting, says he was pressured by police to withhold his testimony.

Veronica Jones says she witnessed someone fleeing from the scene of the shooting, but was told by police that unless she testified against Mumia she would be forced to serve a long jail sentence.

What's more, a man named Arnold Beverly has confessed that he was the person who shot Faulkner. Beverly stated that he and another man were hired by a group of cops and mobsters to kill Faulker because he was causing them problems by interfering in their illegal activities. Beverly said that it was another police officer, not Faulkner, that shot Mumia. Beverly also stated that he was wearing a green army jacket on the night of the shooting.

Ballistics evidence is nonexistent. Mumia was found with a gun the night of the shooting, but he was licensed to carry it. Police never ran any tests on the gun to see if it was fired or on Mumia's hands to see if he had fired a gun. Different police reports make different claims as to the type of bullets found in Mumia's gun. A fragment from one of Faulkner's wounds and a medical examiner's X-ray of Faulkner's body have disappeared.

There is no reliable evidence connecting Mumia to the shooting of Daniel Faulkner, let alone establishing his guilt "beyond a reasonable doubt." By all accounts, Mumia is and has always been a calm and collected person. In fact, his only "record," was that of a former member of the Black Panther Party and a well known journalist who exposed and fought against exploitation and injustice — including the firebombing of the back-to-nature MOVE commune's house by Philadelphia police.

His trial was presided over by Judge Albert Sabo who has sentenced more people to death than any other sitting judge in the United States. During Mumia's trial Sabo said "I'm going to help them fry the nigger." He allowed the prosecutor to argue for the death penalty on the basis of Mumia's former membership in the Black Panther Party.

Mumia's imprisonment has been condemned by a large number of political organizations, artists, unions and educators.

Mumia is confined to a tiny cell 23 hours of each day. He describes it as living in a bathroom. He is denied contact visits with his family and has been punished for continuing to write from behind bars.

Marshall "Eddie" Conway

Marshall "Eddie" Conway, falsely accused of the murder of a Baltimore police officer, has been in prison for close to four decades.

On April 25, 1970, two police officers were fired upon while sitting in their patrol car. One officer was killed and the other was injured. Soon after two men were arrested at the scene. The next day, Conway, a postal worker and member of the Baltimore Branch of the Black Panther Party, was arrested on the (supposed) word of an "unnamed informant" and an officer who arrived at the scene of the shooting and claimed to have seen a third man "at a distance."

Eddie Conway has never been linked by any physical evidence to the shooting. According to police, Conway confessed to a repeat informant that was placed in his cell against his protest (which was made, in writing, to prison guards). The use of such informants was well known to the Black Panther Party, which was subject to attack for years. The third police officer who arrived at the scene of the shooting claimed to have "followed a man who seemed to be acting suspiciously." He originally failed to identify Conway from a set of photos. It was only after he was shown a second set of photos, in which Conway's photo was the only one repeated from the first set, that he identified Conway as the man "acting suspiciously." The "identification" took place in the same station house that Conway was being held in. A lineup could have easily been arranged, but never was.

At the time of Conway's arrest, the Baltimore Branch of the Black Panther Party had already come under attack. Recently released documents show that Conway and the rest of the branch were under constant FBI surveillance prior to his arrest and that the branch was infiltrated with government agents and informants. A mass arrest of members the Baltimore Branch took place immediately prior the police shooting on claims that they tortured and murdered an informant. The first of those members to stand trial was acquitted after a mere two and half hours of jury deliberation. The charges against the remaining members were dropped.

At trial, prosecutors relied on the testimony of this informant and the third police officer. Conway wanted to defend himself, but was denied the ability to do so by the judge. On most of the days of the trial, Conway wasn't even in the courtroom. The jury was not sequestered and was no doubt exposed to the inflammatory anti-Black Panther Party rhetoric which filled the local media (and which has since been connected to the FBI's counter intelligence program which had the stated goal of destroying the Black Panthers).

The Cuban Five

The Cuban Five are five men from Cuba imprisoned for long terms in the United States on false charge of espionage.

Anti-Cuban terrorist groups have waged attack after attack on Cuba for close to fifty years, leaving more than 3,000 Cubans, along with several tourists, dead or injured. These groups operate with the full knowledge, and support, of agencies like the FBI and CIA.

Gerardo Hernández, Ramón Labañino, Antonio Guerrero, Fernando González and René González volunteered to come to the United States to infiltrate the terrorist groups in order to prevent future attacks on Cuba, at great risks to themselves.

But far from being embraced as anti-terrorists, the Five were rounded up by U.S. authorities and held in solitary confinement for seventeen months. Their trial was held in an atmosphere of absolute hysteria in Miami, home to the largest number of opponents of the Cuban Revolution in the world. The judge repeatedly denied attorney's motions for a change of venue despite the obvious fact that a fair trial could never be held there.

194

In 2001, after a seven month trial, the five were convicted of four life sentences and 75 years in prison.

The Five are held in separate, maximum-security prisons around the United States. The wives of two of the Cuban Five have repeatedly been denied visas that would allow them to enter the U.S. in order to visit their husbands.

Their trial, and subsequent treatment, has been condemned by groups and individuals in twenty U.S. cities and more than thirty countries, along with the United Nations Commission on Human Rights, Amnesty International, and eight international Nobel Prize winners.

In 2009, the Supreme Court refused to review the convictions of the Five after Solicitor General Elena Kagan filed a brief on behalf of U.S. President Barack Obama requesting that they refuse to reopen the case.

Leonard Peltier

Leonard Peltier, a former leader of the American Indian Movement (AIM), has been imprisoned for more than 32 years on false charges of murdering two FBI agents. He is serving two consecutive life sentences.

In the early 1970's, the tribal leader of the Pine Ridge Reservation hired a group of vigilantes, who referred to themselves as GOONS, to rid the reservation of AIM members and supporters by force. Dozens of people were injured or killed as a result. The FBI supplied the GOONS with information and even ammunition.

In response, a number of people asked Peltier and other AIM members for help. Peltier and a small group of young AIM members set up camp on a ranch inside of the reservation.

On June 26, 1975, two FBI agents in unmarked vehicles drove onto the ranch. They originally claimed they were in pursuit of a man in a pick-up truck. No pick-up truck was ever found. Later, after they found that the truck could not be tied to Peltier, one of the agents changed his claim and said that they were in fact in pursuit of a red and white van that Peltier was occasionally known to drive.

The arrival of the FBI agents frightened residents of the ranch. Shots broke out. Soon a full out shootout was taking place. Before long, more than 150 FBI agents, law enforcement agents and GOONS surrounded the ranch.

After the smoke had cleared, two FBI agents and one Native American boy were dead. The death of the Native American, Joseph Stuntz, has never been investigated.

The U.S. government moved quickly to charge Peltier and two other AIM members (Bob Robideau and Darrell Butler) with the shootings. Robideau and Butler were acquitted by juries who found they acted in self-defense. No charges were ever brought against any of the other 37 people the FBI claimed were involved in the gun battle.

Peltier managed to escape to Canada but was eventually captured in 1976. Peltier was extradited to the U.S. on the basis of affidavits signed by a women Myrtle Poor Bear who claimed that she was Peltier's girlfriend and had witnessed the shooting. In fact, Myrtle had never even met Peltier. She later admitted that she was forced to sign the affidavits by the FBI.

Peltier's trial took place in 1977. The judge refused to allow Myrtle to testify and excluded other evidence which had been allowed in the cases of Robideau and Butler.

A ballistics test showing that the bullets that killed the FBI agents did not come from the gun was initially hidden. Another 140,000 pages of FBI documents concerning the case were also kept out of the hands of the defense and view of the jury.

Three Native teenagers testified against Peltier, though none of them identified him as the shooter. Later, they admitted they were forced to testify by the FBI. The FBI openly admits it paid another woman who testified against Peltier $42,000.

Amazingly, the prosecution admitted during the trial that they did not actually know who shot the two FBI agents. Still, they claimed, Peltier was guilty whether or not he was the one that killed the agents since, according to them, he participated in the shootout.

Peltier has repeatedly been denied parole despite admissions by the Parole Commission that "the prosecution has conceded the lack of any direct evidence that he personally participated in the executions of the two FBI agents."

Peltier's case has won the support of numerous individuals and organizations around the world.

Workers are enslaved, exploited and under attack

"There's class warfare, all right, but it's my class, the rich class, that's making war, and we're winning." - Warren Buffet, capitalist billionaire.

Since the rise of slave-states in ancient times humans have been divided into classes. Different groups of humans belong to different classes depending on their relation to the means of production (the machinery and technology used to create the things people use). Because of these varying relations to the means of production, different classes also have different interests. Classes with opposing interests are always entrenched in a struggle against each other. This is class struggle.

It is through this struggle, and the subsequent evolution of the means of production (improvement of technology, i.e. from the windmill to the power plant) that history has progressed, from the slave-state to feudalism, and from feudalism to capitalism.

Because of the uneven development of the world and the rise of powerful countries, different parts of the world can be in different historical stages of development at any given time. It is even possible for remnants of past historical stages to continue to exist along side the a new historical stage (i.e. feudal property relations and a rural peasantry in the countryside within a capitalist country). Despite this uneven development, capitalism is today the dominate social system in the world.

Under capitalism, those who own the means of production (the rich minority) make up the capitalist class (or bourgeoisie), which is the ruling class. Those who use those means of production to create wealth (the exploited majority) make up the working class (or proletariat).

The working class is made up of those who have no way to earn a living other than working for the capitalists – that is, selling their labor-power (this includes the unemployed who haven't or can't find a capitalist to sell their labor-power too).

Under capitalism working people are wage-slaves. Lacking control of the means of production, they must sell their labor to the capitalist bosses or starve. The capitalists, to whom workers are nothing more than another commodity, make their profits through the purchase of this labor at prices well below its value.

A simple example of this is a worker who assembles simple toys in a capitalist's factory for $5 an hour. The toys themselves are made by combining two plastic pieces, which the capitalist purchases for $1 each. The worker assembles ten toys an hour, so the capitalist has put forward $25 to create 10 new toys. The capitalist then sells the ten completed toys for $3 each, thus bringing in $30. Since the materials the toys were made of cost the capitalist $20, and the hour of labor of the worker cost him $5, he made a profit of $5. That profit came from the exploitation of the worker! The twenty plastic pieces alone were only worth $20. It was the labor of the worker that added value to those pieces, allowing them to be resold for an additional $10. But instead of receiving the full value she created ($10), the worker only receives a fraction ($5), and the parasitic capitalist keeps the rest.

What's worse, the worker who created 10 toys in an hour can only afford to buy 1 of them with the wages she received for an hour of work.

While this is an admittedly basic example, this is how capitalism functions; and this is the role of the working class -- the class that creates all wealth, but receives only enough of it in return to stay alive and continue producing workers -- which makes it the only truly revolutionary class.

The working class has allies, like poor farmers, who also

have interests that are diametrically opposed to those of the capitalists. The vast majority of people on earth are a either a part of the working class or allied with it.

The petit-bourgeoisie (or middle class), is made up of those who own small businesses or serve as managers or administrators for the capitalists. They have no natural allies, and in fact may have interests in common with either of the main opposing classes, though they are more likely to side with the capitalists than with the working class, since they have a stake in capitalism.

Since the capitalist class controls the means of production, they also control society. Of course, they rule in their own interests.

The interests of this ruling class are diametrically opposed to the interests of the working class, which creates all wealth but controls none of it, and its allies. There is a constant struggle going on between these classes: the class war.

Because of varying conditions and contradictions there are times that this class struggle sharpens and explodes into open conflict, and other times when it appears (at least on the surface) that there is no struggle going on at all.

But we even when everything looks "peaceful" it's not.

Society is constantly in motion. The only constant is change.

Throughout our lives we're told things to make us think that society will continue to go on as they are forever. The widespread belief of this falsehood is in the interests of the rulers.

As we explained, the class struggle and development of the means of production continue to push society forward. This is always true, even when it may be hard to tell that any change is happening at all. Remember that empires have lasted over a thousand years in the past, only to fall apart.

In recent history, in most of the world, the ruling (capitalist) class has been waging a one sided war on the working class and its allies. This is because the capitalist class consciously acts in its own interests; while the workers and their allies to a large degree do not. The capitalists do whatever is in their power to keep the working class from gaining consciousness (i.e. promoting divisions amongst us on "racial," ethnic, and religious lines; distracting and fooling us with the media – which they own and thus control; carrying out minor reforms while leaving the root causes of our problems intact; convincing workers to support capitalist political parties; pushing the myths of "national unity" and the disappearance of classes; etc.).

Despite all this, through the continuing class struggle (and especially in periods when it sharpens and explodes into open conflict), the working class and its allies will become conscious of their own interests, and will finally unite and overthrow the capitalists reign of terror.

Of course, the capitalists will not give up their positions of power without a life-or-death struggle. It will be, and has been, a intense fight with tremendous victories and disappointing set backs but eventually, due to the very nature of capitalism itself, we will prevail. The better informed and organized our class the sooner it will be; and the sooner all of humanity will be much better off.

When the capitalist class is overthrown on a world scale and the working class becomes the ruling class, the next historical period will have been reached. It is then that the material basis for a classless society will finally begin to take shape; and the transition toward a free, just, and equal social order will have begun.

Revolution: What it is and why we need it

The situation we're in

It's no secret that we are plagued by a myriad of problems.

Inequality is at an all time high. The richest 500 people on earth now have more than poorest 50 percent of the world population combined.

Despite the fact that the world can produce enough to meet the needs of all, billions suffer from hunger, homelessness, and lack of medical treatment, simply because they cannot afford to buy what they need.

Everyday some 30,000 children die from starvation or curable disease. The number of children under five years old that dies each year is equal to the combined number of children living in France, Germany, Greece and Italy.

Half of the world's population lives on less than 2 U.S. dollars a day. One of every five people on earth has no access to clean water, while three times that number has no access to sanitation. At the same time, 1 trillion dollars – more than double the amount needed to provide everyone on earth with clean water, sanitation, healthcare and education – is spent on advertising.

Of course major problems do not just affect the poorest countries.

Inequality is especially rife in the United States, the richest country in the history of the world … and it's only growing.

While worker productivity in the U.S. has increased 30 percent per hour over the last ten years, wages have not even kept up with the rate of inflation. At the same time, the rich continue to get a lot richer. The share of total income going to the richest 1 percent of the U.S. population has grown from 8 percent in 1980 to 16 percent in 2004. And while ten years ago CEOs earned 30 times as much as the average worker, today they earn around 300 times as much.

In the "land of opportunity," 36 million people are poor by official standards, 43 million have no access to healthcare, and one of every five children lives in poverty.

Today, countless people are loosing their jobs and even their homes with no assistance forthcoming. Meanwhile, the government is bailing out huge banks with tax dollars taken from the very people that are most in need of help!

This is the face of capitalism, a system based on the exploitation of the majority by a small financial elite.

Capitalism is a system of exploitation

As financial reporter Dianne Maley once remarked, "In capitalist society, the only winners are capitalists."

Under capitalism human beings are divided into classes. The main two classes are the capitalist class and the working class.

The capitalist class is a small class made up of those who own the factories, mines, stores, utilities, and means of communication and transportation.

Because the capitalists control the factories, etc., the majority of society's wealth, and the livelihoods of the working majority, they also control society.

The majority of the population belongs to the working class (also known as the proletariat), which is made up of all of us who work in those factories, mines, stores, etc., whether or not we are currently able to find employment. We do not have anyway to make money other than to work for a capitalist for a wage, thus we are wage-slaves.

Workers create all wealth through our labor, but we only receive a small portion of that wealth in return. The capitalist keeps the rest, which is called profit. This process of exploitation is the basis of capitalist society.

The parasitic capitalists' society is organized around their drive for profits at any cost. This leads to wars, layoffs, "out sourcing," and a host of other ills.

Capitalism is not "broken," and it cannot be "fixed"

When working people are exploited, a section of the working class is forced into unemployment, prices increase and wages and benefits fall, and wealth is increasingly concentrated in the hands of fewer and fewer people, it is not because capitalism is "broken." This is exactly how capitalism functions!

When the CEOs of corporations take home huge bonuses while at the same time the rank and file workers under them are forced to take pay cuts, capitalism is working exactly as it is supposed to. Capitalism is organized to continually create profit for the financial elite. It cannot be transformed – through minor modifications – into a system that benefits the majority. Those who pretend such a change to the capitalist system is possible are either confused themselves or are working to confuse the rest of us by building illusions in this wretched system.

The very best we can hope for under capitalism are a few gains here or there. Such gains – such as shorter work days – only come out of serious struggles and in special circumstances. Even then, all such gains are temporary and can - and eventually will be - rolled back. The fundamental character of the system itself cannot be changed. This system must discarded.

What we need is a new kind of system – a truly

democratic system – organized to meet human need.

Proletarian democracy

Democracy literally means "rule by the majority." How can such a thing exist under a system in which a small elite class controls society and the resources within it while the majority must sell themselves to a boss by the hour just to survive?

Despite the rhetoric of some politicians looking for votes, the working class has no representatives of its own among the various capitalist parties. These parties differ only in their view of how the capitalist class should rule, not *which* class should rule.

Going into a booth every few years and selecting which representative of the capitalist class will serve as the head of the capitalist state is not democracy. In a real, proletarian democracy we would all decide together how society should be run.

To create such a democracy, we must break away from the circus that is "mainstream politics" under the multi-party capitalist dictatorship.

Only revolution can bring about genuine, lasting change

The only way society can be changed in the way that it needs to be is through revolution.

The elite which currently rules society will not just give up its power because we ask them to. History has shown that fundamental change can only be brought about through the revolutionary transformation of society.

Those of us who work, as well as those of us who want to work but are not given the opportunity, make up the vast majority of society, yet we are excluded from power. We must organize ourselves to take power out of the hands of capitalist parasites so that we can wield it ourselves in order to create the kind of society we want and need.

The working class is weak right now, as a result of the many defeats we have suffered, but we are on the rebound. Capitalism is falling in on itself. All over the world working people are getting together and standing up for themselves. Once again the word revolution is on the lips of millions. The more of us that rally together, the better our chances.

So what are you waiting for?

Socialism and Modern Cinema

The Baader-Meinhof Complex: A deficient portrait of the RAF

The Baader Meinhof Complex, a German film directed by Uli Edel, attempts to tell the story of the RAF (Red Army Faction or Red Army Fraction depending on the translation), a group describing itself as an "urban guerrilla" that operated in Germany.

The title of the film alone betrays its approach to the subject. The group depicted called itself the RAF. It was the German press that labeled the group the "Baader-Meinhof Gang" in an attempt to portray it as a non-political criminal outfit.

The founders of the RAF saw themselves as a section of an international movement actively fighting against imperialism. They didn't expect to take power or have a strategy for doing so. They viewed their actions as attacks which would draw some of the attention of the imperialists away from the forces fighting against their domination in places like Indochina and Latin America.

There is much to be criticized in the RAF's politics and actions, but *The Baader-Meinhof Complex* doesn't give a complete enough picture of them to serve as the basis for any real discussion.

While a few references are lightly interspersed throughout the film, no real focus is given to the brutal imperialist war lead by the U.S. in Viet Nam, the occupation of key positions in the German government by former Nazis, the export of guns to bloody African dictatorships by the German imperialists, the repressive actions of the west German state against dissidents or the outright lies meted out by the capitalist media – all of which served as the background for the formation of the RAF.

The RAF arose in a "democratic" west Germany governed by a "Grand Coalition" of the Social Democratic Party and Christian Democratic Union with a former Nazi at its helm, in which the Communist Party was outlawed, radicals were gunned down in the streets and individuals with "unacceptable politics" were blacklisted from jobs. This is not brought out in the film.

The closest thing to an explanation of the RAF's motives and politics *The Baader Meinhof Complex* offers are snippets of political statements written by Ulrike Meinhof, a left wing journalist and original member of the group, and a few pieces of dialogue from a police commissioner who states that terrorism can only be prevented by the elimination of poverty in the Third World.

While important facts and events are ignored, too much attention is given to episodes of violence and infighting.

Large segments of the two-and-a-half-hour film are dedicated to the RAF's bombing campaigns and dramatic gun battles between the group's members and police in pursuit. Predictably, the police stories that the RAF members always shot first, and without provocation are presented as unchallenged fact.

Little is done to show how the group was able to continually draw members into its ranks and gain the sympathy of a large number of Germans. Instead, excessive focus is given to arguments and break downs among the group and its members. Bitter disputes are shown in full detail.

In the latter part of the film, RAF members Ulrike Meinhof, Andreas Baader, Gudrun Ensslin and Jan-Carl Raspe are shown having killed themselves while in prison. In reality, the circumstances of their deaths are still very much in question.

208

Ulrike Meinhof is shown having committed suicide after becoming ostracized by the rest of the RAF prisoners. But this tale of her separation from the others is simply a theory cooked up without any concrete proof. Indeed, many continue to believe she was killed by the German state, and for good reason.

The films also shows defense attorneys smuggling weapons into the prison for Baader, Ensslin and Raspe to use on themselves if they so chose. When the three prisoners were found dead in their cells, this "premeditated suicide" explanation is what was provided by German officials. But later tests showed that it would have been impossible for Baader to have shot himself at the angle that would have produced the fatal wound at the base of his neck. On top of this, the left-handed Baader had powder burns on his right hand while Raspe had no powder burns at all. In spite of all this, and more, the official story is never questioned.

A film that purports to depict historical events must be held to a high standard. At the very least, it should stick to the known facts. Instead, *The Baader Meinhof Complex* presents a flawed picture in a quest to represent the RAF as nothing more than a band of hopeless romantics with guns completely isolated from reality.

The acting in *The Baader Meinhof Complex* is superb, but it's not enough to rescue the film from its own inadequacies. The same can be said of the film's fine cinematography.

In their attempt to create a historical "action film" acceptable in modern capitalist society, the creators of *The Baader Meinhof Complex* produced a film that falls flat.

Everlasting Moments: A film in the service of the status quo

Rather than capturing the essence of the tumultuous times which it portrays, *Everlasting Moments*, a Swedish film directed by Jan Troell, is dull, dry and drawn out.

Based in early 20th century Sweden, the film follows the working class Larsson family through its ups and downs.

Maria Heiskanen plays Maria Larsson, a housekeeper and mother of seven broken down by her work, her abusive, lying, alcoholic husband Sigge (Mikael Persbrandt) and the banality of domestic servitude.

The Larsson family is plagued with contradiction. Sigge is a loving and carefree one minute and violent and demanding the next. He's saddened immensely by his addiction to alcohol, but yet still unable to shake it. Religion and social pressures keep Maria trapped in this seemingly endless cycle, even when she wants to escape.

Impoverished and concerned with the well being of her family, Maria tries to sell a camera she won in a lottery to a Danish photographer (Jesper Christensen). But when the photographer sees the one picture Maria has taken, he urges Maria to keep the camera and shoot more, even giving her the materials she needs.

Maria has an on and off attraction with the camera and the photographer (although she never gives in to the temptation to act on it). At one point, she sets up a makeshift studio in her undersized apartment and becomes a popular photographer, drawing the contempt of Sigge, whose ego is bruised by her independence.

In some of the best scenes of the film, Maria uses her camera to help one mother accept the death of a daughter and another to see the beauty within her Down's syndrome stricken child.

For his part, Sigge becomes swept up in the emerging labor movement. A hard working dockhand, he becomes convinced of the need for socialist revolution through a combination of life experiences and conversations with fellow workers. But it is not his only focus. When Sigge gets involved in a militant strike on the docks and is falsely accused of carrying out an explosive attack in support of it, he is forced to reveal that he was having sex with a barmaid to prove his innocence.

Not enough attention is given to the rising tide of working class militancy of the period. Such a long film could have easily spent more than the few moments it did on the suicide of Sigge's best friend, an active anarchist who hung himself out of despair. And what's worse, after that event we don't hear any mention of the proletarian struggle at all.

Eventually, the Larssons move to an old house in the country and Sigge opens his own transportation business that quickly grows. Maria is shown taking the first and last picture of herself. She died soon after, we're told, content of the life she'd lived.

Everlasting Moments does a good enough job of depicting the life of the Larsson family, and the acting is strong and believable. But in the end, the film serves the status quo with its moral that everything will eventually work out if you just hang in and bear whatever misery you are faced with.

Because of that, the film looses whatever worth it may have otherwise had. After all, the point is not simply to observe the world as it is, but to change it

The Goods fails to deliver

The involvement of a plethora of well known comedians isn't enough to save *The Goods: Live Hard, Sell Hard*, a comedy directed by Neal Brennan.

The Goods revolves around a failing used car lot in California owned by an aging salesman played by James Brolin. The lot is staffed by a group of unsuccessful salespeople played by Tony Hale, Charles Napier, Ken Jeong and Jonathan Sadowski.

While Jeremy Piven seems like the perfect choice to portray Don Ready, the fast-talking traveling car salesman called in to turn things around, he comes up very short on laughs.

His cohorts, played by David Koechner, Kathryn Hahn and Ving Rhames, don't fare any better.

It's not that Piven and company don't try. The film is littered from beginning to end with punch lines and gags. The problem is that they just aren't funny.

Most of the "jokes" come at the expense of workers, women and homosexuals.

In what has to be the most difficult to watch scene, the staff of the car lot is provoked by a nationalist "inspirational speech" and anti-Japanese slurs to carry out a mob attack against an Asian-American salesman. After the attack comes to an end, the perpetrators admit to committing a hate crime but plan to defend themselves with the false claim that the Asian-American came at them with a samurai sword. For his part, the victim of the attack (Jeong) agrees to dismiss the whole thing, saying, "Actually, I'm Korean."

A cameo appearance by Will Farrell and a boy band spoof by Ed Helms add little.

Similarly, the obligatory love interest that arises between Ready and the daughter of the car lot's owner (played by Jordana Spiro) fails to rescue the film in any way.

Watching *The Goods*, one gets the feeling that the writers may have intended the film's more over-the-top aspects to serve as some form of social commentary. If that is indeed the case, they definitely missed the mark.

But even if, on the other hand, their goal was simply to illicit a few cheap laughs, they still fell short.

The Goods could have been something much more. There was no lack of comedic talent and the used car business, marked as it is by fierce competition, predation and deception, is ripe for parody. Unfortunately, *The Goods* simply doesn't deliver.

Little courage in film portrayal of the Heroic Guerrilla

Director Steven Soderbergh has produced a fairly straight-forward, if uninspired, film in *"Che,"* a two-part presentation of Ernesto 'Che' Guevara's participation in revolutionary wars in Cuba and Bolivia.

The first part of the four-hour, 18-minute film depicts the Argentine-born Ernesto "Che" Guevara's participation in the revolutionary war in Cuba, which ousted the bloody-dictatorship of the U.S.-government and mafia backed Fulgencio Batista. The film progresses with the rag tag group of guerrillas as they make their way across the island, gaining support, recruits and victories. Events from Che's initial meeting with Cuban leader Fidel Castro in Mexico through his last battle before victory are accurately portrayed. Throughout the fighting, we are continually brought forward to Che's historic speech at the United Nations in 1964, in which he exposed the U.S. government, which "is not the champion of freedom, but rather the perpetrator of exploitation and oppression against the peoples of the world and against a large part of its own population."

The second part of the film depicts the guerrilla war initiated by Che and a group of his comrades in Bolivia, aimed at toppling the military dictatorship that existed there and paving the way for the construction of socialism. Despite a drawn out introduction which aptly demonstrated Bolivia's location in the heart of South America, those not familiar with Che's ideas may not realize his continental strategy, which was to start in Bolivia with a group of internationalist guerrillas who would, upon gaining enough strength, branch out into the surrounding countries and initiate similar struggles. Using different cameras and filming styles from part one, Soderbergh and company do a good job of recreating the struggle. Most of the events that contributed to Che's defeat – from the monumental betrayal by the leader the Communist Party of Bolivia Mario Monje (Lou Diamond Philipps), who refused to help the struggle as promised and instead actively worked against it, to the treachery of the Argentine artist Ciro Bustos (Gastón Pauls), who drew identifying pictures of all of the guerrillas after being captured by the Bolivian army – are covered. While most fight scenes are realistic, the portrayal of Che's capture in battle is lacking.

While some will undoubtedly argue that film is too long, it could hardly have been otherwise. The historic episodes portrayed in the film deserve serious attention. A condensed biopic of the Che's extensive revolutionary career could not have done it justice.

A better criticism would be to question the exact moments and events that Soderbergh decided to focus on. Noticeably absent from the film were any depictions of the general strike that sealed the Rebel Army's victory and their victorious ride into Havana. Further, there was no mention of the U.S. government's role in Che's execution. While outside the scope of the film, brief overviews of Che's life both before meeting Fidel Castro and during his time in the Cuban government would have been helpful.

Helpful too, both for audiences and the film team, would have been filming the first part of the film on location in Cuba. Of course the blockade that the U.S. government has maintained against Cuba for decades prevented that.

Benicio del Toro is fitting as Che, though he is unable to muster the energy or replicate the depth of the fallen revolutionary.

Demian Bichir does a fairly good job as Fidel Castro, but he lacks the charisma of the Cuban leader. Other actors do good jobs of portraying their respective characters, but Spanish speakers will notice differences in their accents. Catalina Sandino Moreno, who plays the Cuban Aleida March (Che's second wife), maintains the accent of her native Colombia throughout the film. Many others portraying Cuban revolutionaries carry the accents of their native Mexico.

As was the case in his previous film "*The Good German,*" Soderbergh fails to properly develop the characters in "Che" – an unforgivable mistake in a film based on well documented events and historical figures.

In the end, Soderbergh remains too far outside of the main character. Unlike Che, he fails to take any risks. While he doesn't obscure the facts (and briefly allows revolutionary theory and practice to be described from the perspective of revolutionaries themselves instead of the capitalist rulers and their mouthpieces – a rare feat in post-blacklist cinema), he also avoids taking up Che's cause: the cause of humanity.

Thankfully, Soderbergh's film didn't reflect his belief that revolutionary war is "a type of war that can't be fought anymore," or star Benicio del Toro's ridiculous assertion that today "revolutionaries can use elections and other nonviolent methods to promote change."

Sorderbergh has stated that he "wanted to show day-to-day stuff – things that have meaning on a practical level and on an ideological level, but that, from a narrative standpoint, aren't necessarily in support of some goal" to show "what it might have been like to be there." In that he succeeded.

"Che" does a sufficient job of portraying Che and his participation in the Cuban Revolution and guerrilla war in Bolivia. But little courage was shown in making the film, which is very regretful. "Che" was sufficient, but it could have been much more.

www.ingramcontent.com/pod-product-compliance
Lightning Source LLC
Chambersburg PA
CBHW072246310526
45795CB00011B/162